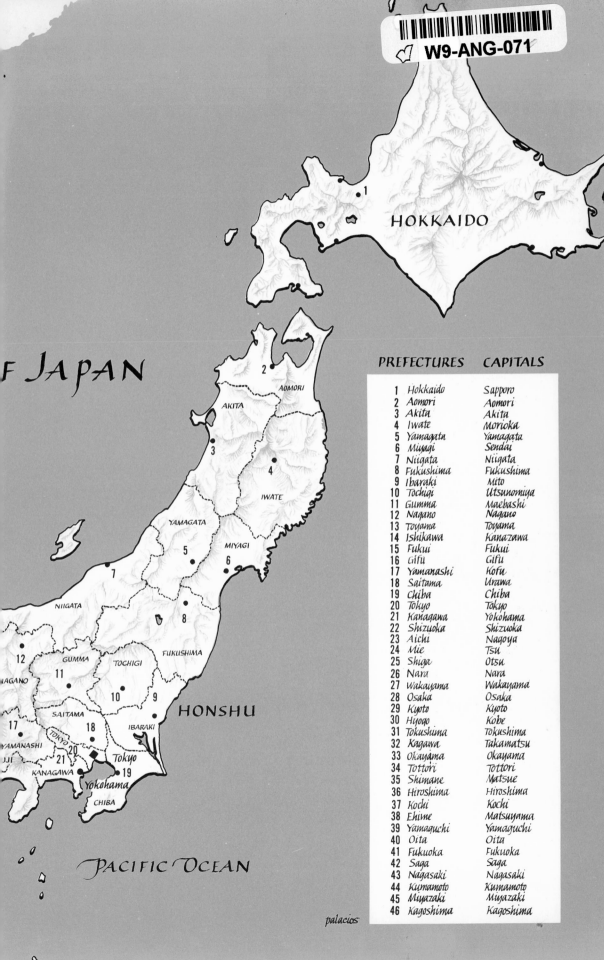

W9-ANG-071

F JAPAN

HOKKAIDO

AOMORI

AKITA

IWATE

YAMAGATA

MIYAGI

NIIGATA

FUKUSHIMA

GUMMA

TOCHIGI

NAGANO

SAITAMA

IBARAKI

HONSHU

YAMANASHI

TOKYO

KANAGAWA

Yokohama

CHIBA

Tokyo

PACIFIC OCEAN

	PREFECTURES	CAPITALS
1	Hokkaido	Sapporo
2	Aomori	Aomori
3	Akita	Akita
4	Iwate	Morioka
5	Yamagata	Yamagata
6	Miyagi	Sendai
7	Niigata	Niigata
8	Fukushima	Fukushima
9	Ibaraki	Mito
10	Tochigi	Utsunomiya
11	Gumma	Maebashi
12	Nagano	Nagano
13	Toyama	Toyama
14	Ishikawa	Kanazawa
15	Fukui	Fukui
16	Gifu	Gifu
17	Yamanashi	Kofu
18	Saitama	Urawa
19	Chiba	Chiba
20	Tokyo	Tokyo
21	Kanagawa	Yokohama
22	Shizuoka	Shizuoka
23	Aichi	Nagoya
24	Mie	Tsu
25	Shiga	Otsu
26	Nara	Nara
27	Wakayama	Wakayama
28	Osaka	Osaka
29	Kyoto	Kyoto
30	Hyogo	Kobe
31	Tokushima	Tokushima
32	Kagawa	Takamatsu
33	Okayama	Okayama
34	Tottori	Tottori
35	Shimane	Matsue
36	Hiroshima	Hiroshima
37	Kochi	Kochi
38	Ehime	Matsuyama
39	Yamaguchi	Yamaguchi
40	Oita	Oita
41	Fukuoka	Fukuoka
42	Saga	Saga
43	Nagasaki	Nagasaki
44	Kumamoto	Kumamoto
45	Miyazaki	Miyazaki
46	Kagoshima	Kagoshima

palacios

JAPANESE FESTIVALS

HELEN BAUER & SHERWIN CARLQUIST

JAPANESE FESTIVALS

1965

DOUBLEDAY & COMPANY, INC., GARDEN CITY, NEW YORK

Library of Congress Catalog Card Number 65–19899
Copyright © 1965 by Helen Bauer and Sherwin Carlquist
All rights reserved
Printed in the United States of America
First Edition

CONTENTS

PREFACE

No longer as remote nor as difficult to understand as it once seemed to the Western world, Japan has much to offer that is only gradually being exposed to those who speak or read English. We hope you will find *Japanese Festivals* a key to discovery of many aspects of this endlessly interesting culture.

Festivals are a particularly suitable goal for the visitor—or reader—because they present Japan on two levels, and one may take from these as much or as little as one wishes. First, the visual aspect of festivals is invariably charming and compelling. Elaborate costumes having a rich sense of design can be enjoyed for their own sake. Secondly, the historical and cultural aspects of Japan are played out in these festivals, much as though they were moving stages on which the story of this nation is told. Japan's background, history, and civilization are so complex that only a few dedicated scholars can be said to have mastered them, but we believe that you will find, as we have, that each festival has a message that can be absorbed in a rewarding fashion.

Neglect of Japan's festivals by the westerner has been no fault of his. Little information has been available in English, and our experience in Japan has proved that only a handful of foreign visitors have been shown the way to Japan's incomparable major festivals and that often none at all are present at some of the very appealing lesser festivals. We sincerely hope that this neglect will end, for Japanese festivals merit attention and are particularly convenient for the traveler. As our CALENDAR OF JAPAN'S FESTIVAL YEAR indicates, they take place at every season of the year and in all parts of the country. We believe that no other country offers events of the magnitude, number, and brilliance of Japan's festivals and we offer this book in the hope that your visit to Japan will be much richer than you had expected.

If you visit Japan, you will find that festivals provide a convenient frame for an itinerary. Also, you will find that local information is helpful. Exact dates of festivals are somewhat variable because of weather or other local conditions, and you will need information as to the precise place in a city where they occur and whether reserved seats are available. The Japan Travel Bureau, the Japan National Tourist Organization, and other travel or information agencies will be helpful. Some cities have a city information office (Kyoto has a particularly good one) that has a list of the events of the week, a valuable aid to the English-speaking visitor.

If you use this book in Japan, you may find that festivals do not correspond exactly with the dates we indicate. With Japan's growing modernization, some customs and observances are changing somewhat or even disappearing, notably in the relatively new atmosphere of the city; in the more stable and classical environment of the mountain and farming areas, especially in northern Japan, they tend to be preserved. That Japan has preserved its hundreds of festive customs as well as it has is amazing, and with a reasonable amount of inquiry and patience, you will be amply rewarded. Some festivals disappear (or are temporarily suspended) for reasons quite unpredictable, but only rarely does this happen. More importantly, occasional celebrations of a non-annual nature appear. For example, a magnificent outdoor No play festival in Osaka marking the three-hundredth birthday of Japan's chief author of No plays occurred in 1963, and many other "once-only" festivals are held from time to time.

In writing this book, we have been the beneficiaries of the eager and generous help so characteristic of the Japanese people. We have enjoyed the hospitality and inspiration of the Hiroshi Murai family of Ashiya, who opened their home and their enthusiasm for their country to us. Mr. Kiyoaki Iwamoto of Kobe, who has lived with us in Santa Barbara as a graduate student, has been of invaluable help in translating original Japanese material and editing.

The Japan National Tourist Organization in Tokyo and the New York office of the Consulate General of Japan proved very generous in offering photographs, acknowledgment for which is given here and elsewhere in the book. The ideographs on chapter headings were made by Mr. Nobuyoshi Aoyama of Kobe, and our appreciation is hereby expressed to him. As always, we must thank the many Japanese people without whose help we would not have seen nor appreciated Japan's festivals.

Special credit is hereby given to Mr. Yukinaga Tomioka, Karatsu Municipal Office, and Mr. Michizane Moroi, Karatsu Kanko Kyokai (Tourism Office), Karatsu, Kyushu, for their generous help in securing material about their city and the famous Okunchi Festival held there.

JAPANESE FESTIVALS

日本の祭

Chapter 1–DISCOVERING A FESTIVAL

Travel often yields pleasant and rewarding surprises, and so it was one summer day in Japan when, returning from viewing the famous old Byodoin Temple near Kyoto, in a car whose driver spoke only Japanese, we became stalled in the Uji-Momoyama region. The narrow streets of the town were choked with automobiles, and crowds of people had hopelessly snarled all forms of transportation. "What's going on here?" we asked the driver in Japanese, expecting to be told that it was another of the numerous accidents that plague the narrow, twisting byways of Japanese towns. The answer instead was "Matsuri," and this single word impelled us to tell the driver to park the car. We crammed extra film into our pockets and elbowed our way into the crowd of spectators. Even though this was our initiation into seeing a *matsuri*, we knew that any festival in this enchanting land is not merely a celebration, carnival, or promotional occasion but is history itself pouring into the street, with rich traditions of great variety brought to life in unforgettable pageantry.

As with almost all Japanese festivals, the focus of this particular one was a portable shrine or *mikoshi;* the festival was a religious celebration sponsored by a Shinto shrine. The crowds of onlookers at Uji were witnessing an event that might seem curious to the Occidental: the carrying of a shrine to the accompaniment of "Wasshoi! Wasshoi!" chanted in the time-honored way. The ritual honored the local deity, whose spirit was enshrined in the sacred *mikoshi,* and the procession through the streets enabled the people to be blessed. The *mikoshi* was a miniature temple ornamented with *torii* (brass devices) and bells and draped with purple silken cords—decorations quite unfamiliar to the westerner; their origins have become lost in time and probably are unexplainable even among the Japanese. The stout wooden staffs that ran through the base of the *mikoshi* served as handles much like those of a litter, so that the heavy shrine could be lifted to the shoulders of the dozen or more men. The *mikoshi*-bearers wore clothes appropriate to the strenuous work—short white trousers and short *happi* coats—and each wore a *hachimaki* or sweatband, an article still in evidence at festivals although vanishing from general use in Japan.

The progress of the *mikoshi* was spurred on by the beating of a *taiko* (drum), which was echoed by the pounding feet of the *mikoshi*-bearers on the hard-surfaced street. As the *mikoshi* teetered down the street, at times veering from side to side and threatening to overturn, it was followed by a tiny one, almost toylike. This bell-shaped *mikoshi* was not heavy, for it was made of gaily-colored cardboard and paper. Children toddled along slowly behind it, the parents admiring the bright red, blue, and yellow costumes, miniature versions of the adult *mikoshi*-bearers. The faces of the children had been powdered and rouged, heightening the doll-like quality so admired by the Japanese.

Discovering a Festival

As the *mikoshi* passed by, the crowd closed in behind and followed to a prearranged point where the *mikoshi* were set to rest on a wooden cart. The adult *mikoshi*-bearers were rewarded for their work. Underneath a broad tent, ladies in festive kimonos handed each one a *bento* (box lunch), nicely made of cryptomeria wood and containing such delicacies as rice balls, bits of seafood, seaweed, and pickled vegetables. The townspeople bought food from vendors and while they exchanged talk about the participants and the bright decorations of the *mikoshi*, parents of the children posed their little ones beside their *mikoshi* and photographed them.

All year long in almost every province there is a festival, fete or fair of some kind being celebrated, either in a populous city or rural area, in an imposing temple or small village shrine, for no people in the world are so festival-minded as the Japanese. Despite the many similarities among village festivals, some are unique. For example, on the evening of October 22, the villagers of Kurama (near Kyoto) and their neighbors gather to celebrate the exciting Hi Matsuri or Fire Festival. In the narrow, solitary street, bonfires piled high with gigantic roots brought from the nearby forest are set ablaze. The village is "beneath the sign of the sacred fire" and, according to popular belief, no serious accident can occur on this particular night that climaxes the celebration.

Soon after dusk, people who have thronged to Kurama enter into the exuberant gaiety of the occasion as torches of all sizes are lighted and the chanting of the rhythmic, meaningless "Sai-rei! Sai-ryo!" begins to fill the air. Children carry small torches (*taimatsu*), most of them made of twigs bound in bark; even babies, under the guidance of their parents, are permitted tiny torches, which they clutch in their chubby little hands. Young men, sixteen or upwards, carry huge man-sized torches, some weighing a hundred pounds or more, some so heavy that several men struggle to keep them upright. A spectacle of brilliance is produced by

14

Frenzy is the keynote at Kurama's Hi Matsuri, where participants seemingly risk conflagration of the town with the furious procession of torches.

the many burning pyres along the street that leads to the mountain slope and by the myriad torches with their licking tongues of flame that shower sparks into the night. The pulsating rhythm of the chants and the constant clapping of hands seem to kindle excitement in the crowd as the torch fires come perilously close to them or their flimsy houses that line the street. Fire is a purifying element, according to Shinto teachings, and there is a belief that no harm will come on this night regardless of the danger. Young men wearing the scantiest of clothing climb a nearby slope to secure the *mikoshi* in which deities are supposedly enshrined, usually represented by a mirror. Near midnight, when the "gods descend to earth," people appear to sense the solemnity of the festival. Suddenly, the disorganized, shrieking torch-bearers form into two orderly rows on either side of the steps leading to the shrine by the mountain slope. Then, from beyond the gateway, appear two enormous gilded, lacquered, sacred *mikoshi,* decorated with silken fabrics, golden bells and, on top, the divine

A *mikoshi* in search of a festival. This small sacred *mikoshi* resides in the shop of a *mikoshi*-maker in Tokyo. Soon it will be the treasured article of a town festival somewhere in Japan.

emblem—the phoenix. The phoenix seems to flap its wings wildly as the *mikoshi* cant perilously from side to side during the dangerous descent. It seems the enshrined spirits are restive and wish to do the guiding themselves. Lest the *mikoshi* get completely out of control, village maidens tug on ropes attached to them, keeping them in balance. Girls participate in the belief that this service insures easy childbirth. Excitement mounts high as the bearers keep time to the shouting, seeming all the while to put their entire strength and heart into the task.

The villagers of Kurama probably could not tell the origin of this festival except to explain that their fathers and grandfathers had such a rite. Thought by some to be a test of virility or something like an initiation upon the occasion of a boy's reaching manhood, today's celebration has lost this meaning, if it once existed.

After the *mikoshi* pass through the river of people, the noisy crowd relaxes into a solemn, quiet mood and, by the light of the torches, watches groups of dancers perform *kagura* (sacred Shinto) dances. It is long past midnight and the reception to the gods has ended. The *mikoshi* are returned to a building provided for them and there they will remain until October of the following year. Torches are extinguished one by one; some people take pieces home with them to be relighted during the ensuing year should there be the necessity to dispel trouble of any kind. Bonfires are reduced to smoldering coals and acrid, smoking heaps. People gradually return to their homes, and there is a mysterious haunting quietness in the long, lone street of Kurama, with no sound but that of the foaming torrent that runs along one side of the narrow valley.

Curiously, the growth and modernization of a city do not crowd out festivals; if anything, celebrations become more elaborate. Tokyo is not only a recent city; it has been renewed and completely modernized several times after earthquakes and war. The expansive commercial empire of Japan centers on Tokyo, and factories and office buildings arise continually. Today, Tokyo looks and sounds like any city in the world and is just as crowded, which is appropriate for the world's largest city. Modernization does not necessarily carry with it complete destruction of the past, however. The Japanese realize that the past is not a single occurrence but is manufactured every day. All traditions were new once, and if they are carried on they must coexist with later innovations and ways of life. The Japanese see nothing unusual in boarding a streamlined subway train to get off at Ueno Station in order to enjoy the view of cherry blossoms in front of a pagoda. Nor is there any reason to be surprised to hear, beneath the rumbling of an overhead train, the beat of a drum announcing the approach of some traditional procession. This may be only a group of young men carrying a portable shrine containing the presence of some deity, or a solemn procession of Shinto priests in elegant robes on their way to a shrine, or a group of marching district elders wearing silk robes with family crests and big straw hats upon which are perched pink paper flowers.

Along the lower section of the city is the wide and always crowded Sumida River with barges and boats of every description. In this part of the city are innumerable warehouses and markets, suppliers of Tokyo's millions. Every year in this area by the Ryogoku Bridge, on the third or fourth Saturday night in July (although temporarily suspended at present) is held a fireworks spectacle, Ryogoku Kawabiraki. In times past, the fete was held earlier (about June 1), the day when the *ayu* or sweetfish season began, and the event was called *kawabiraki* or "opening of the river." The celebration has never had any religious significance but serves to attract people to the river to enjoy the cool evening breezes. A more mercenary reason is the stimulation of business in the area.

Fires released from barges moored in midstream light up the black, oily waters in a fantastic manner. Boats lighted with thousands of lanterns float down the river, some carrying geishas who sing and play on samisens. People crowd housetops and line the riverbanks and bridges to watch the pyrotechnics display. Fireworks explode across the dark sky. When the evening has cooled somewhat and the last spark has sputtered out, the watchers reluctantly turn home.

Japanese festivals are anything but simple; they take many forms, from the dipping of *mikoshi* into the sea at Enoshima to the magnificent, sophisticated Gion Matsuri of Kyoto with its huge *hoko* and *yama* floats. It is at times like this when a city pours its spirit of history into the streets for all to enjoy. No place in Japan is without some occasion to relive, some moment of splendor in its long history, some reason for gratitude. People appear to feel the need to appease or commune with the gods or the souls of generations gone by, to seek protection and guidance.

Festivals have been celebrated in Japan for centuries. The Aoi Matsuri in Kyoto, for instance, has been celebrated since the sixth century, except for some turbulent years in its history, and the Tenjin Matsuri in Osaka since the year 949, with a few years of abstention. Farmers have conceived and observed rites and festivals of their own since ancient times. Some festivals were originated in court circles by an aristocratic society, others by the warrior class, while some have been developed by peasants and merchants; many have a religious origin. The folk faith of today has its roots in the pantheistic past, when natural objects were personified as deities and when the vicissitudes of nature were attributed to the actions

18

Two instruments often included in festival processions are the large drum
(above) and the gong (below). Carried by two participants, these instruments
are laden with elaborate painted wooden decorations.

of gods. Prophetic signs, divination, incantations, and symbolic meanings were developed, many of which became entrenched in the faith and customs of the people.

Chinese culture exerted an overwhelming influence on early-day Japan and affected the rites and festivals through the years. The court and nobles, who were the principal shapers of Japanese culture until modern times, adopted many Chinese celebrations. Among those that still survive are the New Year's events, Boys' Day, and Tanabata. To this day, Chinese legendary figures and decorations and the lion and dragon dances are features of Japanese celebrations.

Discovering a Festival

The rise of the merchants sparked the birth of trade events. The *yabuiri* holiday for apprentices (January 15), the *chugen* or midsummer gift-giving, and the use of fireworks in celebrations were begun by townspeople. Farmers conceived rites according to their beliefs and needs. Flower-viewing picnic parties under blossoming cherry trees were begun by the nobles and adopted by the common people. They are still important palace events, and the emperor holds cherry-blossom-viewing parties in the spring and chrysanthemum-viewing parties in autumn for members of the diplomatic corps, government, and civic leaders.

The word *matsuri* means "worship" or "service" and, as originally conceived, applied to offerings of food, music, and dancing after solemn ceremonial services. Even today, the most joyous time of the year in any town or village is the annual festival of its Shinto shrine. This is the time, established in antiquity, when the enshrined deity descends to earth, a day marked by solemnities and general rejoicing. The precincts of the shrine become the scene of music and dancing, of robed priests, and of merchants' booths ranged along the approaches to the shrines. Surrounding all is a swirling crowd.

The best way to realize the hold that Shinto has on Japanese life is to mingle with the dense crowds that throng the shrines and temples on holidays or festival days, especially in outlying areas. Although formal celebrations are held at night, the festive parts take place both at night and in the daytime. Every district in the country has its *ujigami* or local guardian deity and each shrine has a festival day once or twice a year or oftener. In preparing for the *matsuri*, considerable money and effort are involved. The entire village or district, for example, is decorated with lanterns, essential to all festivals. Among the most important features of any festival of note are costumed processions. *Dashi* (festival floats or carts) are pulled through the streets, accompanied by traditional music and singing. Many families hold merry parties at home during the major festivals that last for several days. Business often is suspended and people devote themselves to enjoying the occasion, away from their regimented existence and the cares of life.

While there are almost as many festivals as there are shrines, few Buddhist festivals are held; most are of Shinto inspiration. In Buddhist festivals, the activities are usually performed by priests rather than by parishioners.

Many *matsuri* are local, but others are observed country-wide, in an unbelievable variety of ways. (See Chapter 15: Calendar of Japan's Festival Year.)

Discovering a Festival

Old customs and ideas, charming as they are, are brought into conflict with the new and are opposed by those with a more scientific and practical approach. This is especially true between the older and younger generations; and between the city-dwellers, with their more advanced way of life, and those in country areas who cling to older ways and dependency on "unseen forces" to bring to fruition the results of their labor. There is satisfaction in knowing that, despite modernity and influences from other countries, "old ways" may still be found in abundance in Japan. Although there are modifications, it is unlikely that many of the treasured customs, such as the festivals, will ever be dislodged.

COMMUNITIES CELEBRATE

Chapter 2 – TENJIN MATSURI, OSAKA

If one could see only a single Japanese festival, the Tenjin Matsuri would be a good choice. It has the elements of the simplest and oldest festivals, all the good fun that creeps into a Japanese celebration, and even some curious alien elements. When we saw the festival on July 25, 1963, the parade was headed by a United States Army band, and the festival boats in the river portion of the festival were emblazoned with advertisements for a popular beer and other products, evidence of commercial sponsorship of the boats being used. Thus, Japanese traditions have a way of renewing themselves in strange and unexpected ways.

The Tenjin Festival dates back to 949 A.D., when the people of Osaka sought relief from diseases prevalent in hot summer weather. Each Osakan took to the Temmangu Shrine a piece of paper cut into the form of a human being and, while Shinto priests of the shrine intoned prayers, rubbed himself with the paper in ritual cleansing. The papers could not then be tossed aside casually; the faithful carried them aboard boats, sailed to the mouth of the river, and there discarded them.

The Tenjin Matsuri today has a dual aspect: a land procession (*okatogyo*) and a boat procession (*funatogyo*) that takes place on the Dojima River, which runs through the center of Osaka. The Japanese have always placed a high value on health and cleanliness, and the persistence of this festival is understandable.

The festival honors Sugawara Michizane (845–903), statesman, scholar, and poet, to whom the Temmangu Shrine is dedicated. He was the greatest student of literature of his time. After reaching the highest post at the court in Kyoto, he was demoted through the intrigues of a rival to the post of vice-governor-general of Kyushu. After reaching his place of exile (as it was considered at that time), he never left his residence but devoted his entire time to study. He was posthumously deified as Tenjin and thereafter regarded as the god of literature.

The Tenjin Festival begins at the Temmangu Shrine. As you await the procession, the first thing heard is the syncopated beating of a drum.

25

In front of the Temmangu Shrine, where the Tenjin Festival originates and terminates, is a large *mikoshi*, guided by dozens of struggling bearers.

When it comes into view, it is seen to be struck not by one but six men. The drum, about five feet in diameter, lies flat in a cart and the beating of it is directed by a man in striped pantaloons who brandishes a wand with multicolored strips of cloth. The six men, in ridiculous tall, peaked, scarlet caps, bend toward the drum and whack it furiously with a drugging insistence. The fervor of the performance is astonishing, and the drummers continue to perform despite all difficulties. Members of the parade remove the platform of the cart from its carriage, and then teeter the platform back and forth, up and down, side to side, as though to defy the ability of the drummers to remain in place while still drumming in an unperturbed manner.

Next, a man on horseback who wears a scarlet robe and a mask that is

At nightfall, all elements of the procession transfer to huge barges. After floating down the river and back again into the city, they will finally pay homage at the Temmangu Shrine, from which the Tenjin Festival began.

a gross caricature comes into view. Like so many of the masks of Japan, this one combines fantastic appearance and revered legend. It represents a character named Sarutahiko, a sort of supergod who guided all the other gods from the divine land to the islands of Japan.

Those who have seen Chinese New Year's celebrations will find the Lion Dance a familiar performance. As though to signify Japan's great cultural debt to China, this dance has been kept much the same for a thousand years. Two men in pantaloons cavort in such a manner as to shake the stringy-haired mane attached to the mask and to display the cloth hanging that drapes the mask. The mask is held in the teeth of the dancer and with his hands gripping a bar that hinges the jaw of the lion, he clacks

27

the wooden jaws and gesticulates, all this in a symbolic effort to bring good luck and drive away bad spirits.

A car that follows, the *Shojo dashi*, commemorates a No play, *Shojo*. On it is a figure in elegant costume; behind the elegance is the story of a No play that celebrates in ritualized form a well of sake that never runs dry. Next, drawn by a sacred ox, is a cart containing books, a memorial to Sugawara Michizane, the scholar sanctified by the Temmangu Shrine.

As if by way of relief, a group of children follows. These tots have been attired, powdered, and rouged by prideful parents who guide their progress down the line of march and shade them with colorful umbrellas.

Attention is then arrested by a pair of dancers with wide umbrellas, colored paper intertwined through the bamboo spokes; these are whirled and brandished by the man whose steps weave in and out in time to the drum beats. In ancient Japan all dancing was done by men.

Boxes containing offerings of rice and tea for the shrine, a flower basket symbolizing the almost sacred art of flower arrangement in Japan, and finally a group of eight geishas dressed in ancient costume complete this part of the parade. These geishas wear tall caps of black gauze and white kimonos and ride in rickshaws shaded by enormous umbrellas.

The second half of the parade consists of palanquins, carts, and various dignitaries including the supervisor of the procession and the mayor of Osaka. This section is concluded with the *mikoshi*, which represents the heart of the procession, for it is said to contain the spirit of the scholar Michizane and is deified with the name Tenjin.

The third section of the parade taxes the narrow streets through which it threads, for it includes the bulky, extremely heavy *mikoshi*, which are covered with bronze. Borne by strong-bodied men who strain beneath the poles attached to the *mikoshi*, the portable shrines veer down the street, being set down to rest from time to time by the earnest bearers. Far from being a chore, bearing such a shrine is considered a privilege despite its discomforts. The Japanese man who drives a bus or assembles radios, enjoys being a *mikoshi*-bearer on this important day. While a *mikoshi* stops for a rest, it is fascinating to examine its details: the graceful curves of the roof surmounted by a golden phoenix, a sacred emblem; the various trappings such as the cords, tassels and drapings of orange or purple silk, colors esteemed by the Japanese. Looked at closely, the *mikoshi* reveals many faithful miniature features found in a temple.

For those who wish an additional view of the participants, the evening boat parade offers an opportunity. All who marched in the parade are loaded onto the boats and barges at Hokonagashi Bridge in central Osaka. As twilight falls, bonfires are lighted along the riverbanks and the boats themselves are electrically illuminated. The barges have colored lights and lanterns, sometimes arranged so as to depict fantastic forms. As the barges are towed down the river, one hears the music of Shinto instruments: the *sho,* with its mystical, continuous cluster of notes; the thin melody of the *hichiriki* or nine-holed flute, and the muffled beat of the *taiko* (drum). The barges proceed down the river and back again, for the sacred objects must be returned to the shrine by morning. As night falls, the beating of the drum by the same six men in peaked scarlet caps still resounds. Finally, the sky is illuminated by great bursts of varicolored fireworks, which make flashing patterns across the sky, providing a brilliant conclusion to one of Japan's most varied and ancient festivals.

Tenjin Matsuri, Osaka

Chapter 3–AOI MATSURI
OR HOLLYHOCK FESTIVAL, KYOTO

The world's oldest festival is in Kyoto. Dating from the sixth century, the Aoi Festival has changed little in fourteen hundred years, and combines colorful costuming, chaste elegance, and reverence. It takes place on May 15, when Japan's cherry blossoms have fallen and the irises are yet to flower. The gray and often rainy skies that habitually blanket Kyoto at this time of year make the pageantry of the Aoi Matsuri even more brilliant and evocative by contrast. Legend has it that an excess of rain was responsible for the inception of the Aoi Festival. Excessive flooding in Kyoto spurred the sixth-century residents to petition their gods for abatement of the high waters, and when this occurred, the event led to a celebration that has been repeated almost every year since. As in some Japanese festivals, the customs and dress of a particular period, in this case the Heian, have been adopted for the annual celebration. The name of the festival, Aoi, is usually translated "hollyhock" by the Japanese, but it is probably a different plant, a kind of wild ginger (*Asarum*), having heart-shaped leaves. This plant is evidently now rare, for the leaves used in the 1963 festival were those of the katsura tree (*Cercidiphyllum*), probably because they are heart-shaped also. The function of this foliage in the festival is to be offered to the Kamigamo and Shimogamo shrines as tokens for the gods. The Aoi Festival also is associated with the royal imperial processions that used to make pilgrimages to the two shrines.

The many personages in the Aoi Festival assemble at the *Gosho* (Imperial Palace) and begin their procession at ten o'clock on the morning of May 15. Spectators may purchase seats for viewing the parade at this location, although the long, circuitous route the procession takes to the two shrines offers many other opportunities for viewers.

A feature peculiar to the Aoi Festival is the imperial messenger and his retinue. This group surrounds the large oxcart (*gissha*), its authenticity preserved in its elegant lacquer and squeaking wheels. Draped from the roof of the cart are streamers of artificial wisteria (*fuji*) flowers. The richly ornamented brocades and cavernous-sleeved kimonos of the retinue are characteristic of the Heian period. *Eboshi,* high-backed black hats as shiny as beetles, have curious curled banks of cloth which cover the ears. Unlike helmets, these *eboshi,* the kind once worn by lords and princes of the court, often perch precariously atop the head. Finally, the cart is drawn by a black ox, a venerated beast whose dark color is set off by a brilliant orange silk cover with large silk cords and tassels.

Other eye-arresting items in the parade include great umbrellas (*furyu-gasa*) so heavy that their functional aspect gave way long ago to cere-monial usage. They are garishly covered with artificial flowers, probably peonies, although their gigantic shapes exceed anything produced by na-

Aoi Matsuri or Hollyhock Fes-tival, Kyoto

A central feature in the Aoi Festival is the appearance of this enormous, sumptu-ous cart, decorated with wisteria blossoms and drawn by an ox led by ropes of orange silk.

ture. The serene lady who is carried on a litter proves to be the representation of a princess whose lot it was to master the difficult life of a Shinto priestess. Other participants representing members of the imperial family ride in the procession, affording a fine display of equestrian fashions, including the ornate saddles. A program is provided for those unacquainted with the various ranks and costumes of Heian days, a helpful guide in identifying courtiers, guards, warriors, dignitaries, and other participants in the colorful parade. As at virtually every Japanese festival, there is traditional music, played on flutes, gongs, and drums.

東照宮祭

Chapter 4 – TOSHOGU (SHRINE) MATSURI
OR SENNIN-GYORETSU
(PROCESSION OF ONE THOUSAND PERSONS), NIKKO

Everything about Nikko is resplendent, or so say the appreciative Japanese, who have an expression, "Never say '*kekko*' (magnificent) until you have seen Nikko." The assemblage of showpiece buildings is extraordinary, and the visitor will certainly be favorably impressed by the *Sennin-Gyoretsu* (procession of one thousand persons) celebrated each May 17 and 18 by the Toshogu Shrine of Nikko.

The Toshogu Shrine and surrounding buildings and tombs are in the heart of a mountainous, forested region that seems bathed in a super-natural light. Probably the memory of this place, with its serenity and majesty, promoted Shogun Tokugawa Ieyasu, founder of the powerful Tokugawa Shogunate, to request burial there. When he died at seventy-five, in accordance with his will his son transferred his remains from a temporary place in Shizuoka to a simply-built mausoleum in Nikko. His grandson, Tokugawa Iemitsu, who is also buried there, is responsible for the mausoleum seen there today. With the aid of vassals during this feudal period, he expended twenty million yen in the construction and decora-tion of the vermilion-lacquered buildings. Gold was used lavishly, more than a million sheets of it; the finest builders, craftsmen, and artists of the period, thousands of them, were summoned to produce the workman-ship and decoration, the most opulent to be found anywhere. So intricate is the ornamentation of Nikko's celebrated buildings that one or another is always under repair, since constant maintenance is necessary.

In May, 1617, a long procession crossed the sacred vermilion-lacquered bridge that arches the nearby Daiya River, slowly climbed the stairs that led to the long lane of stately cryptomeria trees, and brought the body of the famous Shogun Ieyasu to its royal resting place. In memory of that event, on May 18 each year the Toshogu Shrine, dedicated to him, has

33

Nikko's Toshogu Shrine Festival has the advantage of dense groves of cryptomeria trees which set off parades of men dressed in the curious armor of former
times.

one of the most impressive festival processions to be found in all of Japan.

On the morning of the *Sennin-Gyoretsu,* on May 17, descendants of the
Tokugawa family and selective representatives cross the vermilion bridge
that leads to the shrine and make offerings to the three deities enshrined
there: Minamoto Yoritomo, Toyotomi Hideyoshi, and Tokugawa Ieyasu.*

---

* MINAMOTO YORITOMO (1147–1199): overthrew rival Taira (Heike) clan; laid basis
for government by military leaders; known as the Grand Marshal of the Empire; set up
Kamakura *bakufu* Shogunate based on loyalty between lord and vassals. After several members of his family succeeded him, the Minamoto line came to an end.

TOYOTOMI HIDEYOSHI (1537–1598): sometimes called the Napoleon of Japan because

Splendor added to splendor is one way to describe the appearance of a bronze *mikoshi* in front of Nikko's elaborate Yomeimon Gate.

The spirits of the three shoguns (usually represented by metallic mirrors, as in other shrines) are transferred to three sacred portable shrines and are carried through the famous Yomeimon Gate (Gate of Sunlight) to the nearby Futaarasan Shrine, there to remain until the next day's procession of one thousand persons.

On May 18, tremendous crowds swarm around the Futaarasan Shrine awaiting the historic procession. The clattering of horses' hooves on the hard pathway heralds the first horseman of the parade, which will pro-

---

he made himself master of the entire country; built enormous castles (Osaka Castle in 1584 and Fushimi Castle in 1596); great progress made in all forms of art during this period.

TOKUGAWA IEYASU (1542–1616): founder of the powerful Tokugawa Shogunate feudal system; defeated all enemy factions, readjusted administrative and social structures so well that they survived for two and a half centuries.

ceed down the avenue of cryptomeria trees. A hundred soldiers with halberds march in two lines, accompanied by costumed samurai guardsmen. Because lions are believed to keep evil off the road, a large company of men with shaggy, shaking manes appear. Fifty spear carriers (*yarimochi*) are followed in line by an equal number of men with old matchlock guns and still others with bows and arrows, all supposedly representing men in the service of the shogun. Then come warriors wearing antlered helmets and ornamental, protective armor and bearing bright orange shields. Twelve page boys follow next, dressed in unique hats with animal heads, each representing one of the twelve hours of the day. Men wearing fox masks appear, symbolizing foxlike phantoms believed to dwell in the mountains around Nikko and pledged to watch over Toshogu Shrine and its environs. Probably nowhere in Japan could be found a more august assembly of Shinto priests, some marching with measured step, some on horseback, and many carrying flags and streamers of all sizes, designs, and colors.

The dramatic procession reaches a climax with Shinto musicians marching in time to the heavy tones of great drums and the chiming of bells. They are followed by men carrying stuffed hawks and representing those who trained hawks during the Tokugawa shogunate to catch small birds. Glittering sacred *mikoshi* containing the spirits of the three deified shoguns form a solemn benediction to the long procession.

Before the day's celebration ends and the portable shrines are returned to the sacred palanquin houses of the Toshogu Shrine, some of the crowd gathers around the shrine's sacred stage to see the sacred *azuma-asobi* dance. This would seem to be a logical conclusion to the day's events, but there is still one more, an arrow-shooting ceremony (*yabusame*) reminiscent of a game played during the Kamakura period.

The re-enactment of the rites and traditional customs of another time have opened once more the pages of Japanese history, so that those living will not forget the pomp and ceremony that was so important a part of past periods.

時代祭

Chapter 5 – JIDAI MATSURI
OR PROCESSION OF THE ERAS, KYOTO

Autumn in Kyoto brings with it not merely the famed maple-viewing on Mount Hiei, as leaves change from green into gold and red, but one of Japan's great festivals, the Jidai Matsuri or Procession of the Eras. Curiously, this celebration is a marked departure from the *mikoshi*-bearing that is characteristic of rustic and even sophisticated festivals. Rather, this one displays Japanese history from start to finish. Kyoto can justify a festival of this sort, for it was the capital of Japan for ten centuries and thus can offer a panorama of history rivaled by few other cities.

In 781 Emperor Kammu assumed power. Nara, its stately buildings patterned after those of the Chinese T'ang Dynasty, was the capital and the cultural and spiritual center of Japan. Kammu wished to separate the seat of government from the center of Buddhism, which flourished in Nara. He moved the capital to Nagaoka in 784, a place "remarkable for its beauty." Ten years later it was moved again, to a place nearby. This place was given the name Heian-kyo, or Capital of Peace, and was the origin of present-day Kyoto, which means Capital City. Kyoto remained the capital, except for short periods, and the site of the imperial residence, for a thousand years, when it was moved to Edo (Tokyo) in 1869. The palaces, castles, villas, shrines, and temples attest to the splendor and grandiose abundance of those years. All important personages came to Kyoto on matters of state, and it was the center of court life. There was a continuous flow to the capital of painters, decorators, craftsmen, writers, actors—all of whom were given imperial patronage in a fashion reminiscent of the European Renaissance.

Kyoto celebrated Emperor Kammu's initiation of capitalhood belatedly in 1895, 1100 years later, with the building of the Heian Shrine. The shrine was modeled after the original administration hall of the Imperial Palace but was constructed on a five-eighths-reduced scale. It was dedicated to the first emperor of Kyoto and to the last, Emperor Komei, and the sacred spirits of the two emperors were enshrined within. Thus, the Heian Shrine is known as Heian Jingu rather than Jinja, the Japanese word for a shrine not ennobled by burial of an emperor.

The Jidai Festival begins on October 22 with a special service (*shinko-sai*) early in the morning, when priests offer prayers. Then the spirits of the two deified emperors are transferred from the shrine to two waiting sacred *mikoshi,* to be used in the procession. Outside the scarlet buildings of the shrine, a long column of marchers stand waiting to proceed along the circuitous route to the Old Imperial Palace. Thousands line the streets for the parade, which will pass through the great red *torii* of the Heian Shrine, the largest *torii* in Japan, and to the Palace gardens, thence back to the Heian Shrine.

The chronological order of the eras as represented in the procession is reversed, the Meiji era (1868–1912) heading the parade and the Enryaku

Communities Celebrate

With standards and enormous hats, Jidai Festival participants disport themselves in front of the Heian Shrine.

38

The eras of Japan are on parade at Kyoto's Jidai Festival. Here a group of ancient warriors brings alive the pomp of an ancient military age.

era (782–805) terminating it. Care is taken to assure that every detail of each period is authentic. Before the changes brought about by the Meiji Restoration of 1868, the court nobility of Kyoto had one style of ceremonial dress and the military nobility of Edo had another. This was also true of people of different classes: samurai, priests, farmers, artisans, merchants—each class had a distinguishing style of dress. The shogun, on ceremonial occasions, wore a *hitatare,* a trouserlike garment that extends over the feet and trails behind, giving the appearance of a person walking on his knees. His headgear (*eboshi*), a brimless hat worn with two cords under the chin, was bent to the right side, while the military man wore his bent to the left. The ordinary warrior class, for full dress, wore a *kamishimo,* a rather stiff, two-piece kimono-type costume with flaring shoulders. A formal coat (*haori*) was the full dress preserved by custom for the common people.

The two sections of the procession in which women have a part consist of court ladies in garments of richly colored and designed brocades. The shogun's wife wore a fivefold coat in winter, and in summer an unlined coat over which was a loose-flowing gown with ornate embroidery. Among the upper class, a simple black silk gown with family crest was used as full dress; at the waistline was an obi (sash); the undergarment was white. All these styles and many more can be seen in the long, colorful Parade of Ladies of the Eras.

ORDER OF THE PROCESSION

1. MEIJI ERA (1868–1912)

   Royal Army of the period. Young farmers joined with royal forces to bring an end to the Tokugawa Shogunate, which had been in power for three hundred years.

2. EDO PERIOD (1615–1868)

   Procession of the Tokugawa shogun's deputy paying a visit to the emperor. The shogun used to send his deputy to visit the emperor in Kyoto on special holidays and to attend imperial functions. (Here may be seen footmen with spears and traveling boxes, which they toss from one to the other as they march.)

3. LADIES OF THE EDO PERIOD (1615–1868)

   a. Princess Kazu, sister of Emperor Komei, last ruler of Kyoto. At sixteen she was married to one of the Tokugawa shoguns for political reasons. Here she is seen in her wedding dress and veil in the style of ladies of high rank.

b. Rengetsu, famous nun and artist in tea ceremony; a poetess. Teacups with her handwritten poems were highly valued. All money from their sale went to help the poor.

c. Madam Nakamura Kuranosuke, wife of wealthy Kyoto merchant who won costume contests by wearing a simple black silk kimono with white undergarment instead of the usual richly patterned brocades.

d. Madam Kaji, famous for poems, *Kaji-no-ha* ("Leaf of *Kaji*")

and

Madam Gyokuran, granddaughter of Madam Kaji; a painter. She helped her husband to become a celebrated painter also.

e. Yoshino Tayu, woman of the court, famous for her beauty, intelligence, and art work.

f. Izumo-no-Okuni, an Izumo Shrine maiden who in her youth was a dancer and a dramatist. Kabuki partly owes its origin to her dancing.

Jidai Matsuri or Procession of the Eras, Kyoto

4. AZUCHI-MOMOYAMA PERIOD (1573–1614). Overlaps with MUROMACHI PERIOD
    a. Procession of Toyotomi Hideyoshi, shogun general; warlord responsible for uniting the country. This part of the procession represents an event that took place when his son took a retinue to visit the emperor on the occasion of his attaining manhood.
    b. Lord Oda Nobunaga's entry into Kyoto. Oda Nobunaga, son of a minor baron, became one of the most powerful feudal lords of the day. At the emperor's request, he went to Kyoto to repair the Imperial Palace destroyed by warfare during the ten-year Onin War (1467–1477).

5. KAMAKURA PERIOD (1185–1333)
    a. Triumphal entry of Lord Kusunoki Masashige into Kyoto. Emperor Godaigo (1288–1339) plotted to overthrow the shogunate government (*bakufu*). When plot was revealed, the *bakufu* exiled him to the island of Oki in the Japan Sea (1332). The next year he escaped and overthrew the *bakufu*, aided by his generals, including Lord Kusunoki Masashige. This section of the procession shows Lord Kusunoki and his brother, Masasue, as they entered Kyoto to welcome Emperor Godaigo back to power from exile.

6. LADIES OF THE MUROMACHI (and KAMAKURA) PERIOD
    a. Ohara-me, woman of Ohara (near Kyoto) who used to come to the city to sell firewood and charcoal, carrying her load on her head.
    b. Katsura-me, woman of Katsura (near Kyoto), used to go around the streets of the city selling fish and vegetables.
    c. Lady Yodo-gimi, wife of Toyotomi Hideyoshi, shogun general (see section 4a above). Her costume reflects the luxury of the Momoyama period.
    d. Lady Shizuka-gozen, dancer, singer, and a favorite of Yoshitsune, brother of Minamoto Yoritomo, who laid the foundation of government by military leaders that lasted nearly seven hundred years.

7. KAMAKURA PERIOD (1185–1333)

Company of *yabusame* archers. *Yabusame* is the art of shooting arrows from horseback. Under the guise of being contestants in such a game, the men were also warriors. Here they wear hunting garb, quivers, and deerskin leggings.

OFFERINGS TO THE GODS

Communities Celebrate This is the solemn part of the Grand Procession. Offerings to the spirits of the Heian Shrine are carried in exquisite brocade boxes.

ZEN-RETSU (Prior to Procession of Palanquins)

Shinto musicians; children with butterfly wings and an imaginary bird (*karyobinga*) are followed by parishioners in *kamishimo*, the full dress of the ordinary warrior class.

SHINKO-RETSU

There are sacred palanquins in which are the spirits of Emperor Kammu (Kyoto's first emperor) and Emperor Komei (last emperor to rule in Kyoto). Later, the spirits will be transferred from the sacred palanquins back to the Heian Shrine.

8. FUJIWARA PERIOD (897–1185). Overlaps the HEIAN PERIOD

Procession of court nobles. After the middle of the Heian period, the Fujiwara family held all the high offices, but they centered their attention mostly on the arts and luxurious living.

9. LADIES IN THE HEIAN PERIOD (794–1392)

a. Wake-no-Hiromushi, originator of Japan's orphanages; rescued eighty-three orphans and cared for them.

b. Ono-no-Komachi, poetess noted in court circles for her extraordinary beauty.

c. Daughter of Kino-Tsurayuki. By command of Emperor Daigo, Kino-Tsurayuki and other poets collected Japanese poems; the resulting compilation is the most important anthology of Japanese verse ever published (called *Man-yo-shu*).

d. Murasaki-Shikibu, author of a romantic novel written at the beginning of the eleventh century (Fujiwara period); story of life and love in the court circles of that time, *Tale of Genji* (*Genji Monogatari*).

e. Seisho-Nagon, author of critical essays about court life of the Heian era (called *Makura-no-shoshi*).

f. Lady Tokiwa, wife of one of the generals of the Genji (Minamoto) clan. When he was killed, she took her three little sons to the enemy's headquarters. When grown, these same sons destroyed the enemy clan (Heike or Taira clan).

g. Yokobue, lady of the court who fell in love with an Imperial Palace warrior. Because of his family's objections, he became a priest. In the procession, she is on her way to visit her lover.

h. Tomoe-gozen, a symbol of gallantry among Japanese women. Here she is dressed as a male warrior, in the same type of uniform worn when she fought by the side of her husband in battle.

10. ENRYAKU PERIOD (782–805) (Overlaps the NARA ERA, 600–794)

a. Procession of Warriors. The third person on horseback represents General Sakanoue-no-Tamuramaro. When he was subjugating the rebels in northern Honshu (now Aomori Prefecture), he dressed dummies representing men and animals to mislead the enemy. (See Nebuta Matsuri, CALENDAR OF JAPAN'S FESTIVAL YEAR, August 1–7.) This procession shows his triumphal return.

Jidai Matsuri or Procession of the Eras, Kyoto

b. Procession of Court Nobles. Court nobles in full dress on their way to pay respects to the emperor.

c. Company of Archers. Men of the Nara area excelled in archery. Here they are on their way from Nara, the old capital, to the new capital of Kyoto, guarding the imperial procession.

This brings to a close Kyoto's tradition-filled Jidai Matsuri. The full gamut of Kyoto's history through the eras has been played out through dramatic sequences by representative costumes. The return procession may be observed as it winds back through the streets to the Heian Shrine. The spirits of Emperors Kammu and Komei will be transferred back to their sacred places in the shrine. The horses will be stabled and costumes returned to darkened storerooms, to be hidden away from the outside world for another festival day. (See also HISTORICAL PERSPECTIVE, page 213.)

Chapter 6—GION MATSURI, KYOTO

Although the origins of many of Japan's festivals are lost in time, the origin of the Gion Festival is well known—it was a celebration of the abatement of an epidemic. A public health measure may seem a novel reason for a celebration, but the equipage originally devised was picturesque and has been commemorated in the trappings of today's festival.

Kyoto's plague of 869 A.D. caused an enormous toll. Imperial action was taken; a messenger was sent to the Yasaka Shrine in the Gion section of Kyoto with the emperor's order that sixty-six knifelike halberds, each representing a province of Japan, be erected before the shrine as weapons to destroy the disease. The plague abated rapidly, and grateful citizens of Kyoto have perpetuated the health-insuring ritual. Stylized *hoko* floats bear towerlike structures suggestive of the sixty-six halberds. Other colorful floats of the Gion Festival derive from a remedy devised by the head priest of the Yasaka Shrine. Believing that the brother of the mystical Sun Goddess so famous in Japanese tradition was mystically present in the shrine and that he was extremely potent in the amelioration of health, the priest decreed the building of platforms upon which objects sacred to the shrine were placed; these platforms were paraded through the streets. They have become transmuted into the *yama* (literally "mountain") floats of today, boxlike palanquins on which various objects are displayed.

Although processions of these two types of floats are the central feature of the Gion Festival, other events relative to the celebration take place. Between July 1 and 29 the citizens of Kyoto have a welcome preoccupation during the steamy days of southern Japan's midsummer, when brilliant sunshine alternates with sudden thunderstorms.

On the opening evening of the festival, July 2, lots are drawn by which the order of the floats in the parade is determined. On July 8, assembling of the floats begins. Although the floats are exactly the same year after year, they are too bulky to be stored whole and are taken apart following the festival, to be put together the following year. In a sense, they are prefabricated, for they consist of timbers that can be fitted together easily and held together by means of rice-straw ropes. The *hoko* float takes the form of a towering cart two stories high, on four great wooden wheels. Floats in various stages of construction may be seen at the curbs in several parts of the city. As a float is assembled, it soon becomes too high to permit workers to climb onto it from the ground, and a catwalk is built out from an adjacent building. The float is plain and unpainted except for a black lacquer roof, but during the parade of floats its sides will be covered with brocades, tapestries, silks, and various other decorations of religious signif- icance. The tower will be swathed with scarlet bunting like a fantastic conical cap, terminated by various pole- or swordlike devices. Preserving not only the original spirit of the festival but tokens from its manifestations in various centuries, the drapings of the *hoko* include such items as Gobelin tapestries decorated with figures of heroic Teutonic braves and ladies fair. The presence of such decorations in a ritual of ancient Japan is not so inappropriate as one might think; the Japanese wish to celebrate the festi- val in the most colorful fashion, and these pictorial flashes from other lands and other centuries, do blend into the over-all scheme.

Gion Matsuri, Kyoto

Meanwhile, the smaller, boxlike floats, the *yama*, are pieced together. Unlike the *hoko*, the *yama* are carried on the shoulders of a dozen or more men, with poles that extend in front of and behind the *yama*. This means of transport reminds one of the *mikoshi* used in other Japanese festivals, but the decorations are quite different. Although some floats bear temple- like or *mikoshi*-like decorations, others are surmounted by costumed figures from Japanese legends and history, such as Benkei of Herculean strength whose brave exploits bear a close resemblance to those of another legendary hero, the Roman Horatius at the bridge. Each *yama* will have its own theme and its own tapestries and, in addition, pine trees or artificial cherry blossoms (July is well past the cherry-blossom season in Japan).

In the meantime, other events counterpoint the festivities. On July 10, a sacred *mikoshi* is taken from the Yasaka Shrine to the Shijo Bridge across the Kamo River. Here it is given a ritual washing. In the evening of the same day, the faithful of the Yasaka Shrine carry poles bearing lighted lanterns and make a ritual visit to the sacred *mikoshi*, providing a charming spectacle well suited to the warmth of a summer night. These lanterns are forerunners of other events. On the nights of July 11 and 16, preceding the processions on the following mornings, lanterns are strung up on the *hoko* floats. Looking like sails, these gay strings of lanterns are lighted in the evening, providing centers here and there throughout the city where Kyoto's citizens may see and enjoy each *hoko* in the process of preparation for the parade and see the offerings, such as enormous casks of sake, which surround it. The lighting of the lanterns, an event known as *yoi-yama*,

45

is repeated all along Kyoto's streets by lantern-bearing standards erected by merchants.

Before this time, a *chigo*, or page-boy attendant, has been elected to officiate at the festival, much as is seen in the "royalty" of some Western festivals. Although each *hoko* once had its own *chigo*, doll figures now replace them on all the floats but one in the Gion Festival. The one elected *chigo* rides on horseback to the Yasaka Shrine on July 11 and ritually receives a title, as one might be honored by the emperor. The *chigo*, with his elaborate costumes and painted face, is sacred throughout the festivities and may be seen at various places in the city, an attendant cooling him with an enormous fan. Moreover, the family of the *chigo* participates in the privileges of the occasion and may be seen wearing costumes and posing for photographs.

Gion Matsuri, Kyoto

On the morning of July 17, twenty *hoko* and *yama* are readied for the parade through the streets. Nine floats will comprise a similar procession on July 24. Most spectators choose to watch the first parade. As they sit or stand along the streets designated, they cool themselves with fans and ward off the July sun with conical hats. The *yama* and *hoko* start from the various places where they were originally put together, and they will return there when the parade is over. Before they start, special treasures are carried across catwalks to each of the waiting *hoko;* finishing touches are carefully applied to the life-size figures on the *yama* and they begin to move into position for the procession. Because of the height of the *hoko* towers, streets on which there are no electric wires are selected insofar as possible. But on other streets, the wires must be taken down. This is a troublesome task, but one that is willingly undertaken, for Kyoto makes whatever sacrifices are necessary to keep its traditions alive.

Each of the *hoko* has its own retinue, like a machine that must be tended. Long, thick ropes, attached to the front of each *hoko,* are grasped by dozens of costumed men who must pull the unwieldy cart through the streets. The process of pulling the *hoko* is governed by two men, each with a bamboo pole; when the *hoko* is to stop, they signal by crossing their poles in its path. Steering is a problem seemingly not solved by the makers of the first *hoko,* because this process is still carried on by men who carry huge wooden wedges. When a turn is to be made, the wedge is inserted under the front wheel that is on the inside of the turn, leaving the other one free to move.

OPPOSITE:
The commercial spirit mingles in a friendly fashion with the Gion Festival; this street decoration carries out the *yoi-yama* (evening *yama*) theme and advertises one of Japan's leading beers.

47

Each float in the Gion procession has its own theme, matched by the clothing of its attendants. The fan of this man implies a maple-leaf motif (right). Laden with silks, tradition, and formality is the patient child, the sacred *chigo* of the Gion Matsuri (above).

Gion Matsuri,
Kyoto

Each *hoko* is preceded by a group of men in antique costumes having flaring trousers and winglike shoulders; these are replicas of costumes worn at court in earlier epochs. The attendants bear designs on their clothing that identify them with a particular *hoko*. Some wear maple-leaf designs; others have stylized cherry-blossom insignia or other devices that repeat a motif contained on the *hoko*.

"Aboard" the *hoko* are two men in white who stand on a shelf in the front. Holding a thick rice-straw rope with one hand, they each brandish a fan with the other. To the rhythmic beating of drums within the *hoko*, they raise, turn, and lower the fans. The fans are white, with a scarlet circle symbolizing the sun goddess associated with the festival. On the second story or balcony of the *hoko* are musicians, drummers, and flutists. Their music will signal the approach of the *hoko* to waiting spectators and will accompany the strenuous tugging of the two files of men who pull the *hoko*. Attached to the sticks of the drums are richly brocaded blue bands, which hang down the sides of the *hoko*. As the drums are struck in succession, the bands are moved up and down, producing a pattern of motion associated with the drumming.

Finally, a pair of men may be seen sitting on the roof of the *hoko*, clinging to the towering ornament as the *hoko* teeters down the streets and around the corners. The function of these men is to toss *chimaki* to the crowds. *Chimaki* are fascicles of straws, each wrapped in bamboo leaves. Although these contained sweetened rice in earlier years, nowadays they are symbolic; they are much sought after by those who clamor for them. *Chimaki* are said to bring health to the lucky recipient for an entire year.

Alternating with the *hoko* are the cumbersome *yama*. On account of their tremendous weight, their bearers do not hold them up at all times during the procession but cheerfully rest them on the ground at intervals when the parade, which stops and starts, comes to a halt. Indeed, the *yama* bearers can often be seen sitting, chatting, and eating refreshments before the *yama* must be moved a block or so to keep up with the rest of the parade.

At various times during the month-long tenure of the Gion Festival, groups of Shinto adherents say priests may be seen forming for processions at the Yasaka Shrine. Colorful costumes, musical instruments, and recondite festival objects may be seen at these times. The visitor can see the paraphernalia and participants of the Gion Festival to better advantage than at many other Japanese festivals and will certainly want to do as the Japanese do—photograph this curious and incomparable event.

50

FLOATS IN THE FIRST PROCESSION – GION FESTIVAL

(Morning of July 17)

1. NAGINATA HOKO (Halberd Float)
   Chigo or deity's page boy in Shinto robes.

2. KAKKYO YAMA (Faithful Son Float)
   The float depicts a Chinese father and son beside a grave intended for the son, whom he planned to kill because of extreme poverty; instead, the father found a pot of gold in the ground.

3. MOSO YAMA (Faithful Son Float)
   The theme of the float is derived from the story of a Chinese son who searched for and found bamboo sprouts in midwinter to fulfill the wish of his sick mother.

4. HAKUGA YAMA (Hakuga Float)
   Hakuga, the great harp player, destroyed his harp when his best friend died because he thought his friend was the only one who ever appreciated his music.

5. KANKO HOKO (Kanko Barrier Float)
   A long pole on top is surmounted by a crescent moon and there is a mountain on the float; both are symbolic of an old Chinese legend.

6. HOSHO YAMA (Float of Warrior Hosho)
   Represents the warrior Hosho, who broke into the emperor's garden to steal roses for his sweetheart, a court lady.

7. URIDE YAMA (Float of Revelation by Divination)
   The Empress Jingu planned an expedition to Korea but first went to the river for smelt-fishing in search of a sign that would tell her whether she would succeed or fail in her mission there.

8. ASHIKARI YAMA (Float of the Reed Cutter)
   The scene is from a No play, *Ashikari*. The statue of a man who lived in a reed-covered cottage by a desolate seashore is said to be over four hundred years old.

9. TSUKI HOKO (Float of the Moon)
   The crescent moon on the pole of the float was made in 1811. This float is considered the most elaborate in the procession; contains tapestries from the Ming Dynasty (1368–1644).

10. HAKURAKUTEN YAMA (Chinese Poet Float)
    Hakurakuten, Chinese poet, and Dorin, Chinese priest, here are represented discussing the Zen sect.

Gion Matsuri, Kyoto

51

11. Abura-Tenjin Yama (Float of Abura-Tenjin God)

Dedicated to Sugawara Michizane, court noble and scholar of the eighth century.

12. Niwatori Hoko (Chicken Float)

Circle in triangle on pole is supposed to represent an egg in a war drum, symbolic of the idea that peace has been hidden away like a chicken in a drum but that it could burst forth at any time.

Communities Celebrate

13. Arare-Tenjin Yama (Float of Hailstone Tenjin God)

A fire broke out in Kyoto over four hundred years ago; the city was saved by a hailstorm in which the Tenjin God appeared.

The *yama* (Uride Yama) celebrates one of history's footnotes. Empress Jingu (who is represented here), bent on conquest of Korea, prayed for victory by angling for an *ayu* (smelt).

52

14. YAMABUSHI YAMA (Float of an Ascetic)
Yamabushi, an ascetic, noted that the Yasaka pagoda was leaning and prayed unceasingly that it would be straightened, and it was.

15. KIKUSUI HOKO (Float of Chrysanthemum Water)
From a Chinese legend that says that man may live long if he drinks water near which chrysanthemums grow. Float built in 1952.

16. TAISHI YAMA (Float of Crown Prince Shotoku)
The statue on the float of the crown prince (sixth century) was made by Unkei, artist of the Kamakura period (1192–1333).

Gion Matsuri, Kyoto

17. TOKUSA YAMA (Float of Rushes)
The scene is from a No play and represents an old man whose son was kidnaped and given back to him by a kindly Buddhist priest. Here the priest is seen with a bundle of rushes and a sickle in his hands.

18. HOKA HOKO (Float of Beaming Down)
On the high pole are sun, moon, and stars that cast their light on the world.

19. IWATO YAMA (Float of the Rock Door)
Dedicated to the Sun Goddess, Amaterasu Omikami.

20. FUNE YAMA (Ship Float)
This float is modeled after an ancient ship used by the Empress Jingu at the time of her Korean expedition.

FLOATS IN THE SECOND GION PROCESSION

(Afternoon of July 17)

1. KITA KANNON YAMA (Float of Northern Goddess of Mercy)
This is a sister float of the one that appears last in the procession; dedicated to Koryu Kannon.

2. HASHI-BENKEI YAMA (Float of Warrior-Priest Benkei on Gojo Bridge)
Scene from a No play. Two statues, a boy named Ushiwata and a warrior-priest, Benkei. The boy heard that the warrior-priest attacked people passing over the bridge and he set out to punish him.

3. SUZUKA YAMA (Float of Goddess Suzuka)
The goddess Suzuka destroyed a demon that came out at night and attacked people of the village.

4. EN-NO-GYOJA YAMA (Float of En-no-Gyoja, Ascetic)
Represents a Japanese fable about En-no-Gyoja, the ascetic who had a demon carry stones to build a long bridge.

5. KOI YAMA (Float of the Carp)
   The theme of this float comes from a legend that a carp changed into a dragon and swam up the Dragon Gate Waterfall. This miniature shrine-float is dedicated to a mystical deity, Susano-o-no-Mikoto (brother of the Sun Goddess, Amaterasu Omikami) for whom the Gion Festival is held. All screens on the float are Gobelin tapestries.

6. HACHIMAN YAMA (Float of the War God Hachiman)
   Image of the war god, Iwashimizu Hachiman. The sculptor of the image was Unkei, of the Kamakura period.

7. JOMYO YAMA (Float of Priest Jomyo)
   From "The Tale of the Heike," in which a warrior-priest and Ichirai Hoshi fought on the banks of the Uji River (1180).

8. KURONUSHI YAMA (Float of the Poet-Courtier Kuronushi)
   Dedicated to Otomo-no-Kuronushi, a poet; the idea for the float is taken from a No play, *Shiga*.

9. MINAMI-KWANNON YAMA (Float of Southern Goddess of Mercy)
   Dedicated to Yoryu Kwannon, Goddess of Mercy; sister float of the first one in the afternoon procession.

Although all are called floats, the *yama* are carried and the *hoko* are on wheels and are pulled.

The *chigo,* or page-boy attendant, is always on the first float in the first procession of the Gion Festival, but the order of floats in the procession may vary, since their order in the line of march is chosen by lot prior to festival days. However, each *hoko* and *yama* has an identifying subject and the observer may determine the name of the float by this means.

In the second procession, the Northern Goddess of Mercy is always first and the float of the Southern Goddess of Mercy is last. The order of the floats is previously determined and announced by programs in Japanese and English, which are distributed to those who have purchased seats to watch the processions. For details about location of floats, where to get tickets, line of march, etc., consult the Kyoto information booth in front of the Kyoto station.

OPPOSITE:
With its crew of musicians, the ship float, unique among the Gion Matsuri floats, moves forward to the rhythmic raising and lowering of fans bearing the pattern of the rising sun.

55

FESTIVALS OF THE FAITHFUL

Chapter 7 – BON MATSURI
OR FESTIVAL OF LANTERNS

The Bon or O-Bon Festival has been observed by Buddhist families since Buddhism was introduced into Japan about the year 552. Though it was first celebrated only by the court and noblemen, it soon became popular among all classes as Buddhism spread. Not a national holiday, Bon is generally observed as a three-day celebration (July 13, 14, 15), a time for reunion of the living with spirits of the dead. It is observed as a time of meditation, the primary purpose of which is to perpetuate in memory, to show respect for, and to acknowledge gratitude to ancestors. It is reminiscent of the Christian All Saints' Day, which has been passed down through the years and has evolved into Halloween, celebrated on the evening before the Feast of All Saints, October 31.

While Bon is conceded to be a solemn occasion, there is a decided overtone of joyousness in the idea that dead relatives can return to visit with the living. In the Orient, the dead never seem far away, and Bon commemorates their desire to visit the living. Many rites and events are associated with the celebration, and while details differ according to the locality, the essential features are the same everywhere. Visitors will find interest in events held in city parks but will find celebrations in rural districts especially interesting.

In preparation for Bon, houses and graveyards are cleaned. A trip is made to *Bon-ichi* (Bon market) or *kusa-ichi* (grass market) to buy decorations, food, and offerings during festival days. A visit to a Buddhist graveyard during Bon season will reveal elaborate decorations. Somber branches of the Japanese umbrella pine, *koya-maki* (*Sciadopitys verticillata*) and *sakaki* (*Cleyera japonica*), both sacred in Japan and native only there, can be seen alongside *mochi* (rice balls), fruits, and incense. On the first night of Bon, Ueno Park in Tokyo features garlands of lighted lanterns, appreciated by the milling crowds around lakeside markets. Hundreds of stalls sell flowers, fruits, vegetables, crickets in cages, red fish, dwarf trees (bonsai), and ferns. There are, of course, the inevitable fortune-tellers and sellers of zodiac talismans (*juni-shi*) for good luck.

Bon begins on July 13, a day of thoughtful and pious devotion. As night falls, families flock to the cemeteries with glowing white lanterns designed to light the way of ancestral spirits back to their homes. Other white lanterns left on the graves cast an eerie light over the otherwise dark cemetery, and clouds of incense rise into the night air. In rural areas, especially in mountainous districts, birch torches are carried to the cemetery to guide the spirits. A lantern in front of each home welcomes their arrival. The head of the family kindles a fire, and conversation is carried on with the spirit as if he were a real person in a living world.

In the main room of the house, where the altar (*butsudan*) is placed, a small mat is spread; upon it is put the *ihai*, the record of ancestry, together with appropriate decorations. Around this is placed a miniature leaf fence. On the table a meal for the dead is served in very small portions which, besides the favorite dishes of the deceased, may include potatoes

Branches of the *sakaki*, sprays of evergreen *koya-maki*, rice cakes, fruit, and incense decorate graves during Bon season.

cooked with sesame seeds, eggplant or gourds, sweets, fruits, and cakes. Special food is served to invited guests and friends. In many homes, priests are invited in to chant sutras for the ones listed on the ancestry record tablet.

On the last day of Bon, "farewell rice balls," of flavored gummy rice (*dango*), are offered to the spirit guests to sustain and cheer them on their return to the other world (*meido*). Farewell fires are lit in front of the houses to serve, along with the lanterns, as beacons back to the celestial world. The most important part of the farewell is the launching of little lighted lantern boats. The shores of city lakes are crowded with people who buy tiny square paper lanterns on a boatlike wooden base. Each boat has a little candle that illumines a printed ideograph meaning "service for the myriads of souls in the other world." To make each floating lantern more personal, the person himself or a priest adds the names of those remembered. Then the dimly glowing lantern boats are put reverently into the dark, silent water. Gradually the lake is filled with the lanterns, which bob and blink as they slowly disappear toward the sea. A particularly colorful version of this ceremony may be seen at Matsushima, where the intricate pine-covered islets of the harbor form a charming backdrop to the chains of floating lanterns.

Bon Matsuri or Festival of Lanterns

During the Bon season, presents are exchanged with friends, and merchants give semiannual gifts to their valued customers. Workers are sometimes given the day off the last day of Bon and receive gifts.

A gay and extremely important part of Bon is the *Bon-odori,* a dance intended for rejoicing; it is a dance that provides the most spontaneous outlet for the Japanese taste for music and rhythm. It is best seen in the country districts, where it is considered one of the gayest events of the year, especially for young people, who dance most of the night in the precincts of temples and shrines. Among the most popular dances are the religious folk dances performed in Kosi (Nagano Prefecture), Sado Island (Niigata Prefecture), Tokushima (Tokushima Prefecture) on August 14–16, and Shiraishi-jima (island in the Inland Sea) on August 13–16, but they may be seen to some extent in cities and villages almost anywhere in Japan. *Bon-odori* is a rhythmic dance in which performers, singly and in pairs, assume graceful postures almost like living statues and then sing folk songs. At other times they sway their bodies in unison and swirl faster and faster as the singing, clapping of hands, and stamping of feet and beating of drums increase in tempo. The community dancers and singers seem tireless as they proceed from one folk song and dance to another, each with a different rhythm. In rural districts, so many take part in the *Bon-odori* that the entire community seems to be dancing and singing.

61

Chapter 8 – BUDDHA'S BIRTHDAY

Visitors to Japan are invariably impressed with the number of temples and shrines, attesting to the pervasive influence of religion. In almost every village, no matter how small or obscure, the Buddhist temple is the dominant building.

Buddhism, as the first world religion, spread in all directions from its place of origin in northern India and was introduced to Japan by Korean priests at the end of the sixth century. Buddhism was a far more complex but seemingly more satisfying religion than Shintoism, the old religion. For a time, Shinto was cast into the shade, and by the middle of the seventh century there was an emperor who "honored the religion of Buddha" and forsook the "way of the gods" (Shintoism). Elaborate temples were built, unlike the former simple shrines known to the people; statues of Buddha were erected, such as the most famous single monument in Nara, the Great Image of Buddha, completed in 749 A.D. Many varieties of Buddhism were introduced during subsequent years. Most of the teachings and rituals were so esoteric as to be beyond the understanding of all except the most scholarly. The new religion had little appeal for the common people; the Shinto gods were closer and more familiar to them. Finally, after a series of unfortunate events—warfare, earthquakes, and other disasters—a new type of Buddhism emerged which was called Pure Land Buddhism, for want of a more suitable name. This form of Buddhism taught that the world was in its last degenerate days, that men could no longer solve their own problems or achieve salvation by their own efforts. By appealing to Amida, an incarnation of Buddha, who had vowed to help all men in all circumstances, it was possible to be reborn in a paradise after death. The only thing necessary was for the individual to call upon Amida for help by uttering the phrase *Namu Amida Butsu,* and he would be heard. People seemed to understand this kind of personal religion that gave hope for the future, a chance equal to that of the most learned monk to be reborn into the "unseen world." This, in effect, meant that the present world held no charms; that one could be expected to give up everything, even his life, if necessary. People looked about and, seeing disorder and troubles, could readily believe that this world was an evil place; that Amida's paradise was worthy of achievement. However, people were not willing to forsake their Shinto gods completely; their reliance on them was for the present, not the future, and they needed them to help in the present. They needed help both here and hereafter—hence the simultaneous belief in both Shintoism and Buddhism.

Despite the growth of various forms of Buddhism through the centuries, popular support of Buddhism has now lagged. Many elaborate temples stand as showplaces, deserted except for visitors and during special events

Buddha's Birthday

Although ordinarily somber, Buddhist temples are brightened by miniature "flowery temples." Here girl pours tea over a tiny statue of the infant Buddha.

On Buddha's birthday, Japan's busy pace changes to moods of a religious nature. Offerings are made to Buddha statues throughout the country, such as the great bronze statue of Kamakura.

of the year such as the Bon Festival in July or August (depending upon when a particular area celebrates Bon). Some temples have annual festivals, but for the most part these are spectacles, in which priests perform dances and religious rituals, rather than celebrations in which all the people may join.

On April 8, every temple of note throughout the country commemorates the birthday of Buddha (Sakyamuni) in *Kambutsue* or the "Baptizing Ceremony of Buddha." The ritual, an expression of reverence, consists of pouring sweet tea from tiny ladles over a replica of the infant Buddha. The statue, with one hand raised high toward heaven and the other directed to the earth, represents Buddha soon after birth, when he stood erect, raised his right hand, and lowered his left hand, declaring loudly, "I am my own Lord throughout heaven and earth."

The sweet tea (*ama-cha*) is unlike other teas, because it is made from leaves of a hydrangea (*Hydrangea hortensis*), a bush found mostly in mountainous regions. The leaves are steamed and dried before being made into sacramental tea. The temple offers tea to worshipers to take home so that their religious faith and good health may be perpetuated. Before sugar was introduced into Japan, *ama-cha* was brewed into a thin syrupy mixture as a sugar substitute.

The *Kambutsue* or Buddha-Baptizing Ceremony was first performed at the Genkoji Temple, Yamato Province, in 606 A.D., during the reign of Empress Regnant Suiko (592–628). As a result of the growth of Buddhism during those years, it was only natural that Buddha's birthday should become a popular annual event. Records show that originally perfume was used as well as tea, as it still is in Southeast Asia.

In temple precincts where the celebration is held, the image of the infant Buddha is covered by a temporary, miniature unwalled shrine called *hana-mido* or "flowery temple," the roof and uprights of which are decorated with flowers. April 8 is sometimes known as Flower Day for this reason and also because that date usually marks the beginning of the cherry-blossom season.

In the largest cities, the increased popularity of the holiday is evidenced by thousands of children (usually Buddhist pupils) who dress in gala attire and march in processions carrying flowers. They assemble in Hibiya Park, Tokyo, where their dancing and singing add to the charm of the occasion. In some areas, the flower-bedecked temple, *hana-mido,* is drawn through the streets by a horse or an ox.

FESTIVALS
ON A NATIONWIDE SCALE

Carp kites on poles pay tribute to the boys of the household on May 5 and for the month that follows.

端午の節句

Chapter 9 – TANGO-NO-SEKKU
OR BOYS' DAY FESTIVAL

On the fifth day of the fifth month and for several weeks following, fantastic fish float in the air like kites throughout towns, cities, and villages. Almost every home with one or more sons has a tall pole in the garden or attached to the roof upon which are hoisted carp of brightly colored paper or cloth, one for each son. As the carp fill out and billow in the wind, they appear to swim against an invisible upstream current. The carp exemplifies fortitude, courage, and perseverance in overcoming obstacles. The original intent of the celebration persists even now: to express the hope that each boy in the family will have health, vigor, and success in all his undertakings.

As with almost all Japanese celebrations that date back for centuries, the Boys' Day Festival traces its beginnings to rural custom during the Tokugawa period. Maytime is insect time in Japan and inevitably forebodes crop damage. Farmers formerly frightened insects away by means of bright banners and grotesque figures. Later, these became transformed into representations of warriors famed for their fighting prowess. They were no longer put into the fields to dispel insects but were displayed indoors to evoke for boys of the family the bravery and accomplishments of the samurai warriors, an idea stimulated by the Tokugawa authorities to encourage the martial spirit. Samurai had elaborate festivals, and the merchants and farmers followed their example in a more modest manner. Carp replaced warrior figures about 1772 because the people tended to believe that the indoor display was not sufficient to glorify the festival. The custom of flying tubular carp from poles was rapidly accepted throughout Japan.

In memory of those early days, a tiered stand bearing warrior figures and warrior paraphernalia such as armor, helmets, and leg guards is often placed in the alcove (tokonoma) in the main room of the house. In modern homes these articles are often supplemented by carefully conceived models of Japanese shops, inns, boats, toys—enchanting small objects to be handled

Banners, swords, and miniature sets of ancient armor serve as symbols of bravery and fortitude on Boys' Day.

carefully and preserved from one year to the next. In more affluent homes, there may be a lacquered rack to hold spears, a valued sword with decorated hilt and scabbard, or perhaps a silk banner bearing the family crest.

In the Nara period, *Tango-no-sekku* was designated as the Feast of the Iris (*shobu*), a plant to which magic restorative qualities were ascribed. The word *shobu* sounds somewhat like the word for success, although the word is written with different Chinese characters. Officials even wore wigs of iris leaves, and the swordlike leaves were used to decorate and fend off evil by placing them at entrances, under house eaves, and on the rooftops. In the early seventeenth century, boys had a custom of binding *shobu* leaves into bundles and striking them forcefully against the ground to produce a resounding noise; the louder it was, the greater the satisfaction. Nowadays, on May 5, *shobu* leaves are sometimes steeped in a hot iris-leaf bath (*shobu-yu*) imparting a peculiar fragrance to the water. There is a traditional belief that the iris-leaf bath will drive away illness because it has a miraculous prophylactic quality. Leaves may also be finely chopped and mixed with sake, a drink once enjoyed so heartily by samurai. Special foods prepared for this occasion include *chimaki*, rice balls wrapped in iris or bamboo leaves; *kashiwamochi*, rice wrapped in oak leaves; and *sekihan*, rice steamed with red beans.

Tango-no-sekku or Boys' Day Festival

Since 1945, but completely apart from *Tango-no-sekku* or Boys' Day, the celebration of May 5 as *Kodomo-no-hi* or Children's Day has arisen, and it is a national holiday.

Chapter 10 – HINA MATSURI
OR GIRLS' DAY FESTIVAL

Hina Matsuri or Girls' Day is observed on the third day of the third month of the year, and evidences respect and closeness among family members.

This festival day did not always occur at this particular time of the year, nor was it celebrated in the manner of today. Originally, the holiday was a simple seasonal event, especially in rural areas. It took place a month later (lunar calendar), after the pleasantly warm spring season had begun. For this reason, the occasion was sometimes called the Peach-Blossom Festival (Momo-no-sekku). It was a time for family outings; a time to enjoy the greening countryside and the blossoming trees and, perhaps appropriately, the time to cast crudely-made paper dolls into the rivers and thus dispose of sickness and ill fortune (as in Osaka's Tenjin Matsuri). Sometimes sorcerers were summoned on the "first day of the serpent" to make the paper dolls and perform the rite of transferring known or unknown evils to the dolls and floating them down the nearest stream. In later years the dolls were made of clay rather than paper and were brought into the house and placed on shelves.

The first dolls of ancient Japan were not toys but representations of gods or human beings. The Japanese word for doll, *ningyo*, is written with two characters meaning "human being" and "image." The original *ningyo* were, in fact, to protect against sickness, calamities, or any evil influences. In the country areas, rudimentary dolls of woven straw may still be seen in doorways, at entrances to villages, or tucked away in a corner of a rice paddy. The Gion Festival in Kyoto (July 17–20) has floats decorated with huge dolls, a survival from early days.

After the Edo period, skilled dollmakers appeared, as did competent craftsmen who specialized in creating miniature articles such as chests of drawers, tables, and other toylike paraphernalia related to doll displays. Some of the articles were—and still are—so exquisitely made and expensive that they have become heirlooms and are handed down from generation

On a tiered stand, a royal court in miniature watches over girls who enjoy
their dolls on Girls' Day.

to generation as part of the family heritage. Sometimes a set of dolls and doll furniture is considered a part of the bride's belongings. If there is a new girl baby in the family, gifts from family and friends are very likely to be a set of dolls for later use on Dolls' Day.

The dolls most highly valued are the *dairi-sama*, which represent the emperor and empress, dressed in resplendent ancient court costumes of brocade. They are attended by ministers and other dignitaries, court ladies, and musicians. All are placed on a doll stand (*hina-dan*), which is a five- to seven-tiered shelf covered with bright red material. The *dairi-sama* occupy the place of honor on the top shelf, and below them on successive levels are the *sannin-kanjo*, seven ladies-in-waiting; the *gonin-bayashi*, five musicians; two pages; and three guards. Lacquered dinner services in miniature are laid out on tiny tables in front of each shelf. Other samples of art are tiny chests of drawers, a *hibachi* (brazier), musical instruments, and a palanquin in which dolls might possibly ride. Beautiful as the dolls are, they are meant to be displayed but not handled, since they are valuable. After the festival display, which often lasts the full month, all the dolls and miniature articles are tenderly wrapped, boxed, and put away for the ensuing year.

Because March 3 is also known as Momo-no-sekku, or Peach-Blossom Festival, it is customary to include a branch of peach blossoms, either real or artificial, with the doll display; this is considered an appropriate symbol for happiness in marriage. Peach blossoms traditionally suggest desirable qualities in the feminine character—beauty, gentleness, grace, and serenity.

Hina Matsuri is a time of sociability for the daughters of a family. They invite friends to see the doll display, and the friends are respectful in their admiration of each item on the doll stand. Special foods are part of the happy occasion and include diamond-shaped cakes, fruit-shaped candies, white sake, and tiny bowls of rice boiled with red beans.

Chapter 11 – TANABATA MATSURI
OR HOSHI MATSURI

The Tanabata or Hoshi (Star) Festival is known by both names, but the more popular one is Tanabata (Weaving Loom) Matsuri. It was held on the seventh night of the seventh month of the lunar calendar until the Gregorian calendar transposed it to the precise date of July 7.

Tanabata owes its inception to a whimsical Chinese fairy tale that dates back to the T'ang Dynasty (618–906). The tale involves two radiant stars, Kengyu (Altair or the Cowherd star) and Shokujo (Vega or Princess Weaver star), each set apart on either side of the Milky Way or "river of heaven" (Ama-no-gawa). About the same time each year, Kengyu and Shokujo leave their customary places in the starry heavens and have a joyous meeting. The Princess Weaver, daughter of a celestial king and a skillful and industrious weaver, was weaving cloth for her father's kingly robe one fine day. Looking away from her work, she saw a handsome cowherd tending his cows nearby. Immediately attracted, she laid aside her weaving and went to meet him. They fell in love and determined to marry. The king was not opposed to such a marriage, but his daughter soon became uninterested in her weaving and the cowherd let the cows go astray. This did displease the king, who became so exasperated that he separated the couple and forced them to stay on opposite sides of the Milky Way, with the provision that they could meet each other one night each year. Lacking a bridge across the Milky Way, the Princess Weaver and the cowherd despaired of ever meeting each other until a magpie (*kasasagi*), upon seeing the princess crying, assured her that somehow he would arrange a bridge for her and her lover. At an appointed time, the magpie and his fellows flocked together and formed a bridge with outstretched wings over which the princess crossed to meet her cowherd lover. It is believed that they continue to meet each other every year at the same time and by the same means.

Records indicate that the Empress Regnant Koken (Nara period, year 755) originated the celebration of Tanabata, so-named after the goddess

Sendai, in northern Japan, is a focal point for the celebration of Tanabata Matsuri. Streets are filled with pompons and streamers testifying to the Japanese love of papercraft.

who was supposed to be a clever weaver like Vega. Not until the Tokugawa era (1603–1837) did the people of Tokyo begin to celebrate Tanabata, but, many years earlier, emperors and their families composed poems for the occasion. Eventually, it became the custom to hang strips of paper on bamboo branches and float them down rivers on this festive day. The belief was that if poems or proverbs were written on the strips, good penmanship would be acquired easily. Also, if threads of bright colors were put on bamboo branches, the person had a better chance of becoming a good weaver or seamstress, goals that once held more importance than today. People prayed to the cowherd for good rice harvests and to the princess for skill in weaving, sewing, handwriting and all kinds of arts, music, and poetry writing. People of those earlier days looked up so intently at the Milky Way that the two legendary lovers almost took on reality; stories, legends, and poems by the score were written about them, many of which have been handed down through the years.

Tanabata Matsuri or Hoshi Matsuri

The present-day Tanabata features merrymaking and feasting; it is celebrated with enthusiasm and enjoyment, especially by young people. Offerings of melons, peaches, pears, sweets, and cakes are made to the stars in honor of their annual meeting. The Japanese regard Tanabata somewhat like a children's holiday, and decorations for the occasion are reminiscent of Christmas tree ornaments made by Western children. Bamboo branches are set up in front of houses or garden gates and on them are hung poems written on varicolored strips of paper (*tanzaku*). Papers cut in the shape of a kimono and hung on the branches are offered as a special tribute to the Princess Weaver, and five threads of green, yellow, red, white, and purple (or black) are put there for the lowly cowherd. The day after Tanabata, bamboo branches with their paper-and-string tributes are taken to the nearest stream, where they are allowed to float away with the current.

Tanabata is celebrated in a special way in schools, where children offer to the two stars examples of their calligraphy written on paper strips, in hopes of improving their skill.

Sendai, in northern Japan, observes Tanabata Matsuri with unusual gaiety; there it is one of the most notable events of the year. The festival is held on August 7 (other places observe the holiday on July 7, according to the lunar calendar) and attracts visitors from far and near. Branches of bamboo are set up before every house and are decorated with the traditional strips of rainbow-colored paper and many other glittering oddities of fanciful design. The main streets of Sendai vie with each other in their creations of pompons and streamers, testifying to the Japanese love of papercraft. In the city of Hiratsuka (thirty-nine miles from

Tokyo), an industrial center and fashionable resort, stores have elaborate displays in connection with the Tanabata Festival.

Legend has it that if the day for Tanabata should be rainy, the heavenly lovers as well as the earthly celebrants are disappointed, knowing that the magpies are unable to make the bridge of wings across the Milky Way. The princess and the cowherd must then wait another year for their joyous meeting.

FESTIVALS WITH
A SEASONAL TOUCH

Chapter 12 – NEW YEAR'S FESTIVITIES

The most keenly enjoyed and most widely celebrated events in the Japanese calendar are those of the New Year's season. At the stroke of midnight on December 31, temple bells jubilantly and loudly declare the birth of a new year. With the last portentous reverberation of the 108th stroke of the bells (based on the Buddhist idea that man has 108 cares), evil spirits are dispelled; people acquire a fresh hold on life, with its potential happiness and good fortune; misdeeds are expunged as writing from a slate.

The Japanese word for the New Year is *o-shogatsu*, literally meaning the "just right" or standard, and New Year's resolutions serve to induce prosperity and happiness for the future. Items of unfinished business require attention at year's end, and these include payment of all debts lest one's reputation be impugned. Houses are cleaned, for good fortune is not apt to be found in an unclean home. Foods are prepared or bought from specialty shops prior to the New Year's season so that the holidays may be enjoyed with more leisure and with a minimum of effort. New household items, new clothes, and trinket-covered rakes to "rake in good fortune and prosperity" during the year are popular purchases at this season.

The *kadomatsu* (gate pine) decoration, not seen at any other season, is placed proudly on either side of the front entrance to the house. It may be merely a branch of pine boughs nailed to the entry or gate, but the larger the house the more elegant the arrangement. The *kadomatsu*, consisting of pine, bamboo and, if possible, a sprig of plum blossom, is actually known by the name of *sho-chiku-bai*. All these components are symbols of congratulations and good luck. Pine is strong and rugged and keeps its verdure through the year, a symbol of longevity. The bamboo, straight and unbending, is a symbol of uprightness and rapid growth; it leans with the wind but does not break. The apricot (or plum) often braves the season and puts forth sweet-scented blossoms despite the cold and snowy weather. The *kadomatsu*, with its symbolic use of plants, is placed in front of many houses, in the hope that the year will bring vigor,

A *kadomatsu* (gate pine) decoration, made of pine and cut bamboo, and rice-straw ropes form a characteristic welcome to a Japanese home during the New Year's season.

long life, and strength to all family members. It is left in place until the seventh day, when only a sprig of pine remains as a reminder of the past holiday and as a helpful omen of future days.

Across the top of the gateway or at the door entrance or exit or under the eaves of the house are hung *shimenawa* or sacred rice-straw ropes, made of straws sweet with the scent of the fields. Intermixed with the straw may be found fern leaves (the multiplicity of leaves suggesting expanding or ample good fortune); a small orange, *daidai* (which has the same sound as the Japanese word signifying "generation to generation"); and a small dried or artificial lobster, suggesting old age because of its bent back. The origin of the *shimenawa* is traced to an old myth in which the Sun Goddess, abused by her brother, hid herself in a cave. As a result, the world was plunged into darkness. To coax the Sun Goddess from the cave, other gods and goddesses staged a dance and played music. When she heard the music, she was amused and stole to the cave entrance to investigate, whereupon a powerful god pulled her outside. In the meantime, another god stretched a rice-straw rope across the cave entrance, beseeching her not to hide herself again, so that the world would remain light. Whatever the mythical meaning, the *shimenawa* has been used for hundreds of years to designate the boundaries of a sacred area, whether it be that of a shrine, temple, tree, rocks, or the home, for it is a reminder that the place is clean and exempt from evil spirits.

An important decoration found in the tokonoma or alcove in the main room of the house is the *kagami-mochi* (literally mirror rice cake), made from a hard cakelike dough of pounded rice; it is a small round cake on top of a larger one. Rice cake is a happy omen signifying full and abundant good fortune. The decoration is also called *osonae* or "offering to the unseen." *Kagami* represents *kami* or spirit (mirror) and is one of the imperial regalia of Japan.

Special food (*osechi*), plain and nutritious but not luxurious, is eaten during the holidays, and the first meal of the new year is the most significant and symbolic one. First of all, *wakamizu* (literally "young water") is used to ensure good health for the coming year. To be entirely proper on New Year's morning, the family should rise early, wash in the *wakamizu*, dress in new garments, and sit together as a family for the first meal of the year. *O-toso* (sweet, spiced wine) is served before breakfast as a token of celebration, first to the youngest member of the family and last to the oldest. This ceremony is of Chinese origin. According to traditional belief, if a member of the family drinks *o-toso*, there will be no sickness within the limit of one mile, for it is believed that the drink has the power to destroy evil spirits and invigorate human vitality. The proud father, surveying his family, bows to each in turn, offering the congratulatory greeting "Omedeto," while each in turn responds with a bow and the same expression of good wishes. The special dish of the first meal is *o-zoni* (literally "boiled mixture"), clear or bean-mash soup which may contain small amounts of vegetables or bits of fish or chicken. This is the national dish of the New Year's festivities, partaken of by all classes, rich and poor alike. Many other delicacies are served, including herring roe or *kazu-no-ko* (figuratively "many children"); black beans or *mame* (symbolically "robust"); hulled, baked chestnuts or *kachiguri* (literally "victory"); lotus rhizomes and, of course, kelp or *kombu*, a symbol for happiness. Many of these holiday delicacies are put on a *jubako* or square flat-tiered receptacle of porcelain or lacquer ware and brought out as a special treat during holiday meals or when there are visitors, so that each may take what he prefers.

Festivals with a Seasonal Touch

Friendship is the keynote of the season, and everywhere one may hear the cheery greeting "Akemashite omedeto gozai masu," meaning "The old year has gone; we have a happy new year!" It is considered a time for forgiving, for smiling and genial cordiality to all. Festivities of New Year's Day begin with calls to homes of relatives, friends, and business acquaintances. Sometimes callers merely bow at the entrance and drop a calling card in a tray provided for the purpose. If the caller enters, he is given *o-toso*, sweet sake, and assorted foods before he goes on his way merrily to the next place. If a friend is too far away, greetings are sent by mail. Several years ago, the Communication Ministry devised a plan for increasing revenue by selling New Year postal cards bearing numbers; prizes go to those holding cards with lucky numbers on them. Those who receive such cards arrange them in numerical order and wait for the day when the numbers will be announced, usually about the middle of January. Gifts of all kinds are given out—from sewing machines and bicycles to books of postage stamps. *Oseibo* or year-end gifts are given by landowners to tenants, patrons to shopkeepers, artisans to apprentices, and by others to those to whom they have any obligation. The introduction of Christmas gift giving has widened the scope of gift exchange, especially in cities where department stores (*depato*) have actively fostered Christmas merchandising. (See CALENDAR OF JAPAN'S FESTIVAL YEAR, December 25, page 210.)

Young people find the holidays a time for companionship and amusement. Many choose to leave the cities to celebrate part of the New Year season in snowbound mountains, where they go skiing. Others find excitement in movies, baseball, football, dancing, and other pastimes. Traditionally, many young people enjoy playing *utagaruta*, a unique poem game usually played at this season of the year. Fujiwara Sadaie, a great poet (died in 1242), selected what he considered to be the best poems of his time and made a collection of them known as "Single Songs of a Hundred Poets" (*Hyakunin-isshu*). The poems used in the game of *utagaruta* are divided into two sets, each set having one half of the poem. A reader reads the first half and the game is to pick up the second half from the floor and match the cards, thus completing the poems as fast as possible; the one matching the most poems is the winner. Experts are able to do this almost as soon as the first syllable of the poem is read. The game is exciting and hilarious but requires lengthy practice. *Utagaruta* games are sometimes broadcast by radio, mystifying the Western listener.

Gales of laughter emerge from those competing in a New Year's game of *utagaruta,* the goal of which is to match the last parts of poems with their first parts.

Young boys and men seem to enjoy *tako-age*, or kite-flying, during these carefree holidays, while girls engage in battledore and shuttlecock, a game much like badminton. It is a charming sight to see young girls in gay, long-sleeved kimonos batting the feathered shuttlecocks high in the air and catching them again on their ornately decorated battledores. As a penalty for missing, the player is sometimes dabbed with a bit of ink or powder on her face, but the loser accepts it in the spirit of fun.

A serious side to the holiday season is seen in the throngs who visit shrines to pray for good fortune and health during the year ahead. The most important first visit (*hatsu-mairi*) is made on the first day of the

Festivals with a Seasonal Touch

Half-game, half-rite is the sport of battledore and shuttlecock which girls, clad in fine kimonos, play on New Year's Day. The battledores are highly ornamented.

86

year. If possible, a trip is made to special shrines such as the Grand Ise Shrine. Trains leaving various parts of the country on New Year's Eve are crowded with persons going to the early morning service at the Grand Ise Shrine and others. Local shrines (*ujigami*) have swarms of visitors as soon as the 108 bells are sounded to usher in another year. The Tsurugaoka Hachiman Shrine of Kamakura, dedicated to the God of War, has a tradition of selling at a small cost *hama-yumi*, small arrows with white feathers "to defeat devils." Receivers consider themselves fortunate (about fifty thousand arrows are prepared for the season), since the arrows are supposed to bring very good luck. Those who do not go to shrines to worship pray for their families and country at shrines in their own homes.

The second day of January is also full of events, being the first day for people in all walks of life to start their trade activities. Carts, wagons, and motor trucks are piled high with merchandise and decorated like floats in a parade. These are the vehicles of the wholesale dealers making the first shipments of the year (*hatsu-ni*) in hopes that orders in ample amounts will be placed during the twelve months ahead. For children it is the day of *kakizome*, a day for starting their practice in writing. In the presence of their parents, they write with a Japanese writing brush (*fude*) some phrase of happy significance. They make an effort to write well, for excellent calligraphy on this occasion means a good start in writing for the rest of the year. On this day, carpenters use their tools, and geishas tune their samisens; everyone does all things properly on this day so that all will continue well for the months ahead.

The night of January 2 is important for those who believe in dreams (*hatsuyume*, or first dream of the year); the dream on the first night of the new year may foretell one's fate for the following year. Of all the dreams one may have, the happiest is of ships loaded with treasures, for this portends prosperity and happy days. A dream of a rising sun is equally favorable, as is one about a sea voyage; this foretells good fortune. Normally, one would not want to dream of snakes, but on this particular night such a dream could imply that wealth is in store, and a dream about a sword or knife has a similar interpretation. If one dreams of rain, worries can be expected; moonlight, and there will be a better position in the future, or perhaps fame will come. An earthquake denotes a change of residence; snow portends happiness, and if one is unmarried a dream about ice signifies that an arranged marriage will materialize.

Singers or carolers (*manzai*) dressed in ancient costumes and wearing tall *eboshi* (hats) are known to go to some homes during the New Year's season. They sing happy songs while beating their *tsuzumi* (hand drums). The custom started over a thousand years ago, when artists from China

87

danced and sang in the imperial court to express their season's greetings. At first there were two kinds of *manzai:* those who visited homes of relatives and friends and those who formed professional groups and sang and danced in return for an offering of a few coins by those who gladly paid for the entertainment and greetings. Today's singers are in the latter category, although there are nonprofessional *manzai* in some rural areas. One would not expect to find any *manzai* in the larger cities. *Kakubei-jishi* is another New Year's form of entertainment, developed from the Lion Dance (*shishi-mai*) of Kabuki. Boys of ten to twelve, wearing the head of a lion made of paper and decorated with flowers, go about entertaining.

On the fourth day of January, normal functions of the government are resumed (*shigoto-hajime*), literally "first work of the year"; offices, facto-

In Japan, as elsewhere, renewal is a keynote to New Year's. A ritual accompanies the replacement on January 5 of the great straw-rope (denoting a sacred area) which joins the "wedded rocks" at Futami-ga-ura.

ries, and stores reopen. On the sixth day, firemen give annual acrobatic exhibitions for the citizens of Tokyo and crowds of visitors who come to see this unique event. January 7 is Early Herb Day (*Wakana-no-sekku*), so-named for the rice gruel, made with seven early herbs, served on that day. On January 11, the *kagami-mochi* or two-tiered rice cakes are removed from the alcove and, if not too hard, cut and eaten, a custom once observed by the samurai class. During the days when the *kadomatsu* is in place, the home is said to be *matsu-no-uchi* or "inside the pine." However, the time comes when decorations are regretfully removed; this usually takes place about January 14. Instead of their being tossed into the nearest body of water or being burned in a back yard, a night is designated for burning all holiday decorations in a huge community bonfire. Participants regard the event as one for further merrymaking; they sing songs, roast rice cakes, and tell fortunes. Between January 13 and 16, a holiday (*yabuiri*) is given to those workers who were unable because of their particular duties to take the earlier holiday. January 15 is considered the Small New Year (*Jugo-nichi-shogatsu*), a day for eating, drinking, visiting. This day coincides with Adults' Day, a national holiday, dedicated to young men and women who have reached adulthood during the year past. This does not wind up the season's festivities, as there is *hatsuka-shogatsu* or the January 20 celebration, a day when delicacies are relished for the last time. It is also called *hone-shogatsu* or bone New Year, because the large broiled sea bream (if the family had one), which has been eaten little by little during the holidays, is all gone, all but the bones.

Finally, the season of joy, good will, and renewal of purpose comes to an end. A common New Year song in the Tokyo area originated with an early-day Zen priest who wrote this poem:

> Cranes have a life of a thousand years;
> Tortoises have the joy of ten thousand years.
> May your life prosper and continue
> Longer than the cranes, tortoises and bamboo.

Other songs and poems of the season differ from place to place, but all have the theme of casting away evil influences, of success in all undertakings, of good health, happiness, and long life. All are aware that *o-shogatsu*, the "just right" standard, is a pattern worthy of one's efforts during the months of the ensuing year. (See Chapter 15: CALENDAR OF JAPAN'S FESTIVAL YEAR – January.)

豐年祭

Chapter 13 – RICE AND OTHER FOOD FESTIVALS

Much of the charm of Japan derives from a varied landscape, richly sculptured by green and misty mountains. However, the abundance of mountains and the narrowness of the valleys have cruel consequences to the farmer. The paucity of arable land, only 17 per cent of the Japanese islands, taxes the strength and ingenuity of the farmer. He grows the world's most efficient crop, for no other plant has been found that can yield as many calories per acre as rice. Rice is a monotonously universal necessity of the Japanese diet for breakfast, lunch, and supper and even is regarded with a reverence often transmuted into beliefs, superstitions, rituals, and festivals.

In spring, the paddy fields lie flooded and naked, bare until sowing of the seeds in May. Seeds are prepared weeks beforehand, and various rituals are observed to please the gods. Japanese farmers make much of the cultivation of rice, deeming it their sacred duty to produce as good a crop as possible and yet believing that it is a *kami* or god who gives them a good harvest. The rituals held in the rice-growing regions of the country are the products of ancient days, and the significance of some is lost in time. Although not all rice rituals are identical, they are related in a basic way.

Rice, once used for payment of taxes, allowances, and salaries, was of vital concern to those charged with control over estates. Landholders were responsible for conducting rites and making offerings to the gods to ensure ample rice harvests. In addition to rites practiced by farmers and villagers, great ritualistic festivals were held as official ceremonies. Rites concerned with rice culture extended through the year, corresponding to the seasons and stages of rice maturation.

For a brief period during January there are a few days of relative inactivity among the farm workers. January marks the turning point from winter to spring, bringing with it the resumption of a new cycle in the process of rice cultivation. But even during this period, in the presence of

Because planting of rice seedlings is a critical event in the farm year, the Japanese have crystallized it in the form of ritual rice plantings, as here near the Sumiyoshi Shrine in Osaka (above). The piping of flutes signals the beginning of a ceremony. As priests look on from a platform, a paddy in the precincts of the shrine is planted (below).

the *toshi-no-kami* (year god), people carry out certain rituals pertaining to rice production. The *kagami-mochi* (layered rice cake) is placed in the alcove of the farmer's home or in *sambo* trays, and rice offerings are made at the family altars. If you should pass an empty paddy in January, careful scrutiny may reveal an arrangement of good-luck plants (pine, chestnut, bamboo) to which paper charms (*nusa*) are attached, and beside it, offerings of food to the year god. Between January 11 and the night of the first full moon, about January 15 (lunar calendar), pantomimes are performed showing preparation of the paddy and the rice seeds, planting of the seeds, transplanting of seedlings, "chasing away the bird" (*tori-oi*), and the harvesting.

In the early spring the paddies are made ready for flooding. At that time a bamboo staff is planted in the middle of the irrigation ditch. Attached to it are sacred objects from the nearest shrine. The paddy is ceremonially cleansed by sprinkling water here and there upon it. At the inlet from which the water passes into the paddy, an earth mound is made and into it tree branches are stuck, representing the field god (*ta-no-kami*), together with an offering of freshly roasted rice seeds. Thus, the god of the field is supposed to come into the field with the water (so that water almost becomes a god as well). In February, the emperor officiates in the palace chapel (*kashikodokaro*), imploring divine benevolence for those responsible for the cultivation of Japan's main crop. Then the rice seed is planted.

By June, the rainy season begins; it continues for the next four or five weeks. By this time the rice paddies have changed from the flooded stage to thick, lush patches of vivid green. In June and July, according to district, transplanting takes place. The farming community makes an important occasion of rice transplanting or *taue*. Many districts start the work of transplanting by having costumed young women participate, all the while singing rice-planting songs (*taue-uta*). Again, in some places, Shinto priests are called to offer prayers for a good harvest season.

The actual transplanting takes place when the paddy-field water reaches a proper temperature. Planting is not easy work. Each planter takes in his right hand five or six seedling plants and puts them securely into the muddy soil under water, in straight rows and at regular intervals. Men and women, especially women, spend many tiring hours each day tramping in the muddy, watery fields. With the singing of ritual songs and the performance of other rites, the work seems less tedious and a feeling of significance is lent to the labor.

Farmers and their families feel relieved when the planting of the seedlings in the paddy fields is over, for this signifies the ending of the

A smile denotes a good harvest, a time that is celebrated by rites, dances, and festivals throughout rural Japan.

important stage upon which much of the year's fortune rests. But their labors and worries for the season are not necessarily over. In some years there may be a dry spell or an infestation of insects. In August, there is the arduous task of weeding in the wet fields, walking hour after hour in water heated by summer sun, bending low, and sloshing knee-deep in the mud. Communal rites are offered to offset damage by winds, floods, and drought. During the hot summer months, when the plants require a good supply of water, the *natsu matsuri* (summer festival) is held, honoring the water god. During the typhoon season (210th to 220th day after spring, lunar calendar, in September), the wind god is honored and supposedly appeased by offerings and supplications. Throughout the growing season, scarecrows of all kinds may be seen—strips of cloth, the forms of faces or of people working in the field—all designed to frighten birds away from the ripening rice. Noisemakers or shiny objects are strung across the fields, set in motion occasionally by someone tugging a string. After the harvest, especially in the Shinshu district, scarecrows that have served their purpose well are pulled up from the field and a ceremony is held for them, *kakashi-age*.

Before the actual harvest, when some of the green stalks begin to turn golden in the sun, a small portion of the ripest grain is offered to the gods, while another portion is toasted and tasted by the people so that they may know that their work has been done well. The gods have looked with favor upon their hard work and conferred upon them and their land the blessings due the people for their labor and reverence.

The reaping of the harvest goes on for many weeks, and by the end of that time all is ready for a harvest festival. This is tied in with an *ujigami matsuri* or festival of the village god, to express gratitude for help during the rice-growing season and to send the village god back to the netherworld from which he came. The field god, *ta-no-kami,* is returned to the mountains to become the *yama-no-kami,* the mountain god, and thus, twice each year, in the spring and autumn, there is the ritual of receiving the gods and of *kami-mukae* or "greeting the return of the god." Both the sending off and the welcoming back are related to *kigansai* (prayer for good harvest) and the *niiname-sai* (autumn harvest) festivities, held annually in the Imperial Palace.

While rice is the staple food, and rituals are closely connected with all stages of its culture, rituals also are applied to the planting, growing, and harvesting of wheat. In some cases, the dates and festivals coincide with those of the rice ceremonies. Rites are observed in relation to the growing of other foods too, but not so extensively: potatoes, taro, beans, eggplant, flax, and even the large Japanese radish (*daikon*). Rites relative to hunting and fishing are fully as important to people engaged in those occupations. Success for fishermen in their commercial endeavors is of paramount importance to the millions of Japanese dependent on fish as a basic food. Fishermen lead precarious lives, and because they contend continuously with the dangers and vagaries of nature, they believe strongly in charms and superstitions. They celebrate rites to show gratitude for a good catch, and they offer prayers for a more abundant harvest of fish; there are rites when a boat goes on its first voyage of the season. On April 3, there is a *ura matsuri* or bay festival and an *iso matsuri* or beach festival. Fetes are held spontaneously in fishing communities when there is an unusually large haul (perhaps over a thousand fish in a catch), and with a fete there is great excitement. If luck is bad, fishermen believe that a drinking fete may bring better fortune on the next trip out to sea. (See Chapter 15: CALENDAR OF JAPAN's FESTIVAL YEAR. For representative rice festivals, January 11 and 13; February 2, 17; March 3, 15; April 3; May 15; June 14, 24; October 17.)

Rice and Other
Food Festivals

WINTER   SPRING   SUMMER   AUTUMN

Chapter 14 – SEASONAL FLOWERS
AND OTHER DISPLAYS

As a tourist land, Japan is unique; each season and even each month has its own special attractions. Festivals are had in infinite variety, and the beauties of nature are to be found in all four seasons. The Japanese delight in the four well-defined seasons of the year and find special joys in each one. "My only desire for life is to see the beauties of the changing seasons," wrote the monk Kamo-no-Chomei in 1212.

WINTER (*FUYU*) – *December, January, February**

Winter in Japan can be rigorously cold, except in the extreme south, but the season is usually tempered by warm sunshine and brilliant blue skies. Snow is plentiful in higher altitudes, and Mount Fuji presents a picture of pristine, marblelike splendor. Feathery, swirling snow piles upon rooftops of shrines, pagodas, houses, and trees, creating the fairyland scenes so often depicted on old woodblock prints and scrolls.

For ski and skating enthusiasts there is no more exhilarating season. For those to whom the sports have no appeal but who wish to see Japan and the life of the people during the winter season, there are numerous festivals and special events.

The greatest festival period of the year for the Japanese people is probably the New Year holiday season. People throughout the entire country pause during their extremely busy lives to enjoy a renewal of body, mind, and spirit, which the New Year symbolizes for them. (See Chapter 12 for full description.)

Ume, the Japanese apricot, is the foremost winter flower of Japan. The

---

* See Chapter 15: CALENDAR OF JAPAN'S FESTIVAL YEAR – December, January, February.

An overlay of snow converts Mount Fuji and other Japanese places into special treats for the tourist and photographer.

Items with a symbolic significance are sold during the New Year's season. Here, bright-red *daruma* figures add a mysterious note to the market scene.

blossoms are esteemed because of their delicate fragrance and fragile flowers and because they bring a touch of beauty to the winter scene. The *ume* stands as a symbol of strength and nobility, for, despite the adversity of winter, it pushes forth its bloom before any other flowers of the season. *Ume*-viewing parties, in contrast to cherry-viewing celebrations, are quiet and dignified.

*Festivals with
a Seasonal
Touch*

WHERE TO SEE JAPANESE APRICOT (*UME*) BLOSSOMS

Season	Prefecture	Place	Location
In Kyushu			
All of February	Fukuoka	DAZAIFU	Dazaifu Shrine gardens, forty miles from Fukuoka
In Western Honshu			
Early March	Hyogo	TAKARAZUKA	Takarazuka Apricot Grove
All of March	Nara	NARA	Kataoka Japanese Apricot Grove
Mid-March End of March	Nara	TSUKIGASE	Extends three miles along Nibari River; view from Shimpukuji Temple (Oyama station); regarded as best *ume* grove in the country
Mid-January Mid-February	Wakayama	MINABE	Minabe Apricot Grove; largest in Japan; five thousand acres; extends over hills and valleys in three villages. Thousands from Osaka and vicinity go here for *ume*-viewing
In Central Honshu			
Late February Mid-March	Ibaraki	MITO	Tokiwa Park (or Kairaku-en Park); a noted beauty spot
Mid-February Early March	Kanagawa	YOKOHAMA	Okurayama Park
Mid-February Late February	Shizuoka	SHUZENJI	Shuzenji Park
Late December Late March	Shizuoka	ATAMI	Atami Japanese Apricot Grove (1.8 miles southwest of station)
Late March	Tochigi	NIKKO	Ritsuin Temple garden
All of February	Tokyo	KAMATA	*Ume Yashiki,* garden once owned by Emperor Meiji; old and prized trees
Early March	Tokyo	KAWASAKI	Kuji Apricot Garden
Mid-March Late March	Tokyo	TOKYO	Yoshino (along the Ome line) has a Japanese apricot garden reputed to be among the most picturesque in the country
Late March	Tokyo	TOKYO	Shinjuku Gyoen (Shinjuku Center Gardens), in the southern part of the Shinjuku ward, near the outer garden of the Meiji Shrine
All of March	Tokyo	OGOSE	Japanese Apricot Grove; on Oppe River; highly esteemed grove

SPRING (HARU) – *March, April, May*

In March the days lengthen, cold abates, and the uncertain sunshiny days of spring are followed by an occasional fall of soft, warming showers. Then the *sakura* (Japanese cherry), pride of Japan, the coronation of spring, bursts forth into glorious pink and pinkish-white blossoms. At this season of the year Japan becomes the "Land of Cherry Blossoms" renowned around the world.

Cherry blossoms have a special appeal when they set off a picturesque view, such as the Kintai-bashi Bridge at Nishi Iwakuni, Yamaguchi Prefecture.

The *sakura* is glorified, worshiped, and enjoyed as is no other flower in the world, and it is only natural that the cherry blossom is the national flower of the country. Poets and artists have depicted the loveliness of the blossoms in words and colors through the centuries. *Sakura* is called "the flower of flowers," and when the Japanese use the word *hana* (flower), they mean *sakura*. *Hanami* (flower viewing) means viewing the *sakura* blossoms and no other flower, for this one symbolizes perfection to the people and satisfies their aesthetic taste.

One reason the *sakura* is so highly prized is that the blossom is of such short duration. The Buddhist faith stresses the impermanence of life as symbolized by the blooms. The Japanese soldier was wont to compare his few hours of glory in combat to those of the short-lived *sakura* blossoms. The life of the samurai in feudal days, with his uncertain life in the service of the master, was considered parallel to that of the brief beauty of the cherry blossoms.

During the short blooming season, cherry trees are the topic of the hour. People everywhere discuss the best places to see them, the varieties, the trees of unusual interest because of age, numbers, or sizes. They have become accustomed to dispensing with daily duties during the blooming season; they enter into a gay holiday mood and have *sakura*-viewing parties, with drinks, merry dances, and songs. All through the month of April, the railway cars and other means of transportation are crowded with young and old, rich and poor, on their way to some place noted for cherry-viewing. On the other hand, some prefer to admire the blossoms in a quiet, remote mountain spot or by some riverbank less frequented by people. Some do not care to see great numbers of trees but choose instead the opportunity of enjoying just one choice tree or one branch or even the development of a single blossom.

There are about sixteen principal species of *sakura* but about four hundred varieties. The first trees to flower are the pink-and-white single-petaled variety, the kind generally preferred. Afterward, the double-blossomed varieties may be seen in exuberant abundance in many places for a period of about two weeks.

Cherry-blossom time usually comes toward the end of March in Kyushu; at the beginning of April in western Japan; from the beginning to the middle of April in central Japan, and from the middle to the end of April in the northern sections. Blossoms may be seen in city parks, in temple and shrine gardens, in mountain areas, in pastures, along riverbanks, and in many places throughout the country, depending upon the blooming season of the areas. (See Chapter 15: CALENDAR OF JAPAN'S FESTIVAL YEAR— March, April, May.)

WHERE TO SEE CHERRY BLOSSOMS

Season	Prefecture	Place	Location	
		In Kyushu		
Early April	Fukuoka	FUKUOKA	Nishi Park; 4000 trees	
Early April	Kumamoto	KUMAMOTO	Hanaoka-yama Hill; 500 trees	
Early April	Oita	BEPPU	Kankaiji Spa; 2000 trees	
		In Shikoku		*Seasonal Flowers and Other Displays*
Early–Mid-April	Kagawa	TAKAMATSU	Ritsurin Park	
Late March Early April	Kagawa	KOTOHIRA	Kotohira Shrine; 2000 trees	
Late March Early April	Tokushima	TOKUSHIMA	Bizan Park; 6000 trees	
Early April Mid-April	Ehime	MATSUYAMA	Matsuyama Castle	
	In Western Honshu			
Late March Early April	Kyoto	KYOTO	Heian Shrine; many rare trees. Viewing of blooms at night, an annual event	
Early–Mid-April	Kyoto	KYOTO	Kiyomizu Temple	
Late March Mid-April	Kyoto	KYOTO	Maruyama Park; 6000 trees. Area lighted at night; many visitors	
Late March Mid-April	Kyoto	KYOTO	Arashiyama Park; famous for beauty of setting	
Early–Mid-April	Kyoto	KYOTO	Daigoji Temple	
Early–Mid-April	Kyoto	KYOTO	Ninnaji Temple; aged trees, thick trunks; multiple-petaled; very popular place for viewing	
Early–Mid-April	Kyoto	KYOTO	Hirano Shrine; eighty varieties; popular night viewing	
Early–Mid-April	Kyoto	KYOTO	Zoological Gardens	
Early–Mid-April	Kyoto	KYOTO	Shishinden Garden of the Imperial Palace	
Mid-April	Nara	NARA	Nara Park; 500 trees	
Late March Mid-April	Nara	MOUNT YOSHINO	Perhaps the most famous place of all for viewing; three areas with "1000 trees at a glance"	
Mid-April	Nara	MOUNT YOSHINO	Kokeshimizu Shrine; famous individual tree (Priest Saigyo's tree)	
Early April	Osaka	OSAKA	Hirakata Recreation Park; 3000 trees	
Early April	Osaka	OSAKA	Negoroji Temple; grounds noted for cherry trees	
Early April	Osaka	OSAKA	Osaka Mint precincts; open only during full blooming season	

Season	Prefecture	Place	Location
Early April Mid-April	Shiga	TATEBE	2000 trees
Late March Early April	Wakayama	WAKAYAMA	Kimiidera Temple; 1000 trees
Early April Mid-April	Hyogo	HIMEJI	Himeji Castle; 1000 trees
Early April	Okayama	OKAYAMA	Korakuen Garden; one of the three most famous gardens in Japan
Early April	Shimane	MATSUE	Shirayama Park; 350 trees
Early–Mid-April	Yamaguchi	IWAKUNI	Kikko Park; 3000 trees

Festivals with a Seasonal Touch

In Central Honshu

Season	Prefecture	Place	Location
Early–Mid-April	Tokyo	TOKYO	Ueno Park; 1500 trees (Cherry Hill), up steps to plateau, formerly a daimyo estate
Early–Mid-April	Tokyo	TOKYO	Chidorigafuchi Park; 1000 trees
April 15–20	Tokyo	TOKYO	Koganei Bridge; avenue extends for five miles along Tama River; mostly white mountain cherries with some trees one hundred to two hundred years old; about 4000 trees in the area
Early April Mid-April	Tokyo	TOKYO	Edogawa banks; adjacent to Daikyoji Temple. Favorite picnic spot
Early April	Tokyo	TOKYO	Azuka-yama Park (Opposite Oji station). Oldest flower resort in Tokyo area; noted for single-petal variety blossoms (*someiyoshino*)
Early April Mid-April	Tokyo	TOKYO (area)	Arakawa banks; fifty varieties of *sato-zakura*. Washington (Tidal Basin) cherry trees came from here
Early April	Tokyo	TOKYO	Tama River, near *Yuenchi* (Pleasure Park); noted for ten-mile avenue of trees along bank
Early April	Tokyo	TOKYO	Hinoharu, ninety-three miles from Shinjuku station, Tokyo. Oldest cherry tree in Japan; 1800 years old; 102 feet wide, 37-foot circumference
Mid-April	Tochigi	NIKKO	Rinnoji Temple; two-hundred-year-old tree, prized yellow variety (*kongo-zakura*)
Mid-April	Saitama	LAKE SAYAMA	Sayamako station (Seibu line); 6000 trees
Mid-April	Saitama	NAGATORO GORGE	Nagatoro Gorge; 1350 trees. Area noted for its fantastic rock formations
Mid-April	Gumma	TAKASAKI	Kannonyama Park; 6000 acres of trees
Early April	Chiba	SANRIZUKA	Sanrizuka Pasture; ninety-eight hundred acres of trees (50,000). One old tree, *kasa-zakura* (umbrella cherry), measures fifteen feet around trunk base and has spread of fifty feet

Season	Prefecture	Place	Location
Mid-April	Kanagawa	HAKONE (area)	Gora Spa; 1600 trees
Early April	Kanagawa	HAKONE (area)	Okugawara Spa; 1500 trees
Mid-April	Kanagawa	HAKONE (area)	Kowakidani Spa, 2.1 miles from Miyanoshita; neighboring hills and vales have 30,000 trees
Late March	Shizuoka	ATAMI	Nishikigaura (1.2 miles from Atami, noted for picturesque coast line)
Early April Mid-April	Aichi	OKAZAKI	Okazaki Park; 5000 trees
Early April Mid-April	Aichi	INUYAMA	Inuyama Castle; 6000 trees
Early April Mid-April	Gifu	NEU	*Usuzumi-zakura* or light black cherry; tree is twenty-six feet in girth
Mid-April Late April	Niigata	SHIBATA	Kajikawa riverbanks; 6000 trees
Early April Mid-April	Ishikawa	KANAZAWA	Kenroku-en Park; *kiku-zakura;* many small-petaled chrysanthemum-like blooms. The garden is one of the most noted in Japan. (Others are Kairaku-en in Mito and Koraku-en in Okayama)

In Northern Honshu

Season	Prefecture	Place	Location
Late April Early May	Aomori	HIROSAKI	Oyo Park (or grounds of Hirosaki Castle); 1130 trees
Late April Early May	Iwate	MORIOKA	*Ishiwari-zakura* or "stone-breaking" cherry tree; grows in a gigantic rock and divides into two trunks
Late April Early May	Iwate	HANAMAKI SPA	5000 trees here
Mid-April	Fukushima	FUKUSHIMA	Shinobuyama Park; 500 trees
Late April Early May	Fukushima	KAKUNO-DATE	Ryusenji Temple; drooping-type cherry trees; white blossoms
Late April Early May	Fukushima	MIHARU	*Taki-zakura* or "waterfall cherry"; four hundred years old; has thirty-one-foot girth
Late April Early May	Fukushima	AKITA	Senshu Park; 1000 trees

In Hokkaido

Season	Prefecture	Place	Location
Early May		SAPPORO	Sapporo Shrine; 500 trees
Early May		KAHODATE	Goryokaku; 10,000 trees
Mid-May		NOBORI-BETSU	Noboribetsu; 1000 trees

The list above gives many of the noted places to see cherry blossoms, but it is not complete, for cherry blossoms may be found in many places throughout the country, both in cities and rural areas.

AZALEA-VIEWING

Among other summer flowers that may be seen to perfection in Japan are the azaleas or *tsutsuji*. In mountain districts, such as Mount Aso, wild azaleas are found growing in profusion over wide areas. Good landscape gardens provide fine displays during the azalea season, as do those in many parks and shrine and temple gardens.

Festivals with a Seasonal Touch

WHERE TO SEE AZALEAS

Season	Prefecture	Place	Location
		In Kyushu	
Mid–Late May	Nagasaki	UNZEN SPA	Unzen Golf Course
Mid–Late May	Kumamoto	MOUNT ASO	Grow in great profusion here
		In Western Honshu	
Late April Late May	Kyoto	KYOTO	Heian Shrine garden
		In Central Honshu	
Mid-May	Kanagawa	HAKONE (area)	Kowakidani Spa
Early May	Tokyo	TOKYO	Rijugien Garden
Early May	Tokyo	TOKYO	Azalea garden of Hanayama, 2.5 miles from Tatebayashi station; covers about four acres; 3500 bushes, some said to be over two hundred years old, mostly brought from the mountains of Nikko
Early–Mid-June	Gumma	MOUNT ASAMA	Asama Pasture
Late June	Gumma	MOUNT HARUNA	Ikao Spa, on the shores of the lake
Early May	Ibaraki	OARAI	Oarai-Isozaki Shrine garden
Late May Mid-June	Tochigi	NASU SPA	

PEONY-VIEWING

The peony, *botan,* is much respected and admired by the Japanese, especially by flower arrangers, even though they regard it as a very difficult flower to arrange—as a task possible only to those initiated into the art.

A late spring and early summer attraction is a garden of peonies, long a favorite of Oriental horticulturists (above). Even a city dweller can grow morning-glories in Japan (below). In the middle of the hot summer, boxes of vines can be seen along the sides of crowded streets.

WHERE TO SEE PEONIES

Season	Prefecture	Place	Location
		In Central Honshu	
Early May	Saitama	HIGASHI-MATSUYAMA	Yakyu Tree Peony Garden
Mid-May	Kanagawa	YOKOHAMA	Kamito Peony Garden
		In Western Honshu	
Mid-May	Nara	HASEDERA (near Nara)	Hasedera Temple
		In Northern Honshu	
Early–Late May	Fukushima	SUKAGAWA	Sukagawa Gardens; very old garden with many plants
Early–Late May	Niigata	KOAI-MURA	Acres of peonies, tulips, hyacinths, etc. This area is a chief exporter to the United States

Festivals with a Seasonal Touch

WISTERIA-VIEWING

Fuji or wisteria, with its long, dense, drooping clusters of purplish, pea-shaped flowers, adds a great deal of graceful beauty to the Japanese landscape at this season of the year where it may be seen and admired on walls and arbors, along the eaves of porches, or in public or shrine gardens. Stout vines attain great age, with woody trunks several feet in diameter and having a spread of hundreds of feet.

WHERE TO SEE WISTERIA

Season	Prefecture	Place	Location
		In Kyushu	
Early May	Saga	KARATSU	Maizuru Park
		In Western Honshu	
Mid-May	Hyogo	HIMEJI	Himeji Park
Mid-May	Nara	NARA	Kasuga Shrine gardens
		In Central Honshu	
About May 10	Saitama	KASUKABE	Ushiyama Wisteria Gardens
About May 10	Tokyo	USHIJIMA	Celebrated wisteria; eleven hundred years old; extends five hundred yards
Late April	Tokyo	TOKYO	Kameido Tenjin Shrine
Late April	Tokyo	TOKYO	Hamarikyu Gardens. Tidal ponds are spanned to islets by bridges shaded with wisteria arbors

Season	Prefecture	Place	Location
Late April	Tokyo	TOKYO	Famous Korakuen Garden
End of May	Kanagawa	NISHI-KATSURA	Called "wisteria of the mountain gods"
End of May	Akita	NOSHIRO	Hachiman Shrine; known as Jindai-fuji; is twelve feet in circumference at its base

SUMMER (NATSU) – June, July, August

Seasonal Flowers and Other Displays

Summertime heat comes with the month of June and gradually increases in intensity through July. The long period of rainy weather, which lasts at least three weeks, is welcomed by the Japanese farmer. Interested visitors go to the countryside at this season, for it is the best time to see the busy life in villages and on farms. With the advent of *tsuyu*, as the wet season is called, the age-old, solemn Shinto rites observed in transplanting rice seedlings can be seen in local districts. (See Chapter 13: RICE AND OTHER FOOD FESTIVALS.) Abundant sunshine follows the rainy season. While the temperature is very high in midsummer, seacoast areas provide numerous resorts with pine-fringed stretches of white sand beaches. Alpine peaks challenge mountain climbers. During the early and middle summer season, Japan is practically covered with a rich, velvety verdure. Deciduous trees—cherry, oak, maple, chestnut, birch, and elm—contrast with the deeper greens of the evergreen trees and plants.

Summer events run the full gamut of unique, interesting attractions from fireworks displays to historic processions. (See Chapter 15: CALENDAR OF JAPAN'S FESTIVAL YEAR – June, July, August.)

IRIS-VIEWING

The Japanese iris (*shobu*), an aquatic plant, begins to bloom in the latter part of June, and the season lasts for about three weeks. The iris-flower resort in Horikiri, in the outskirts of Tokyo, attracts large crowds of visitors daily. The gardens may be reached by city tram to Asakusa station, thence to Horikiri by electric train, from which the iris gardens are not far distant. One of the most noted gardens here is the Korakuen Garden in Tokyo, which has been practically intact since the Edo period and is still protected by Tokyo as one of the important seasonal features and a place of historical interest.

The most convenient garden to reach from the center of Tokyo and the best place to view irises is in the private garden of the Meiji Shrine. The

107

As spring changes to summer in Japan, irises grace many gardens. There they may be grown in watery ponds, a method of culture not unlike that of rice. The Japanese iris, unlike bearded iris, has a flat platelike form and varies in color from white to deep purple.

garden is famous for its giant iris blossoms of varied colors. The Meiji Shrine garden is regarded as one of the most beautiful gardens in Tokyo. Emperor Meiji, grandfather of the present emperor, remodeled it according to his ideas and collected iris plants from all parts of the country to add to the garden's beauty. Other celebrated places for iris-viewing are the Heian Shrine garden, Kyoto, and the Ayameike Recreation Park in front of the Ayameike station, Nara.

LOTUS-VIEWING

Hasu or Japanese lotus (*Nelumbo nucifera*) is cultivated throughout Japan. In parks, lakes, and private gardens it is planted for its gorgeous pink or white blossoms, which bloom in the summer season. Farmers cultivate it for obtaining *renkon,* the long, edible rhizomes or stems. In the minds of the Japanese people it is primarily associated with Buddhism and particularly with paradise. "To sit on the throne of *hasu*" means rebirth in paradise after death and is the goal of the Buddhist faith. To view the *hasu* blossoms, it has been customary for the Japanese to have an early-rising party, because the blooms open every summer morning and close when the sun rises high. Some of the best places to see the lotus in bloom are the Heian Shrine garden, Ryoanji Temple garden, Nishi Otani Temple pond, Toji Temple, Shokokuji Temple, Higashi-Honganji Temple, Kyoto; Shinobazu Pond in Ueno Park, Meiji Shrine garden, Tokyo; Tsurugaoka Shrine pond, Kamakura; and the largest lotus pond in Japan at Takada (in the Takada Castle moat), Niigata Prefecture.

AUTUMN (*AKI*) – *September, October, November*

The autumn months in Japan approach perfection, with their clear, crisp weather. Maple-viewing is at its very best; chrysanthemums are abundant. During the season many varieties of festivals and special events take place, particularly in the Kyoto and Tokyo areas. (See Chapter 15: CALENDAR OF JAPAN'S FESTIVAL YEAR – September, October, November.)

The changing of the leaves from greens to hues of gold and red attracts millions of people. From the beginning of October, varying according to the location, the foliage of the maples, sumacs, and other trees is ablaze with gold and scarlet in mountains and countryside. City parks, gardens, and the grounds of shrines and temples afford chances to see individual trees or small groups of trees, if one is unable to venture far afield.

MAPLE-VIEWING AREAS

Season	Prefecture	Place	Location
		In Kyushu	
Mid-October Mid-November	Oita	NAKATSU	Yabakei Valley (1½ hours from Beppu); an area of unrivaled scenery in Japan
Late October	Nagasaki	UNZEN SPA	Unzen-Amakusa National Park; view from Nita Pass
		In Western Honshu	
Early November	Kyoto	KYOTO	Arashiyama Hill. Classic maple-viewing places: Takao, Makino-o, Togano-o at eastern foot of Mount Atago
Late November	Nara	OJI	Tatsutagawa Park (twenty-three minutes by train from Nara)
Mid-October Mid-November	Kagawa	SHODO ISLAND	Kankakei Valley (four hours from Kobe)
Early November	Hiroshima	MIYAJIMA (ISLAND)	Momiji-dani (Maple Valley), especially noted for autumn foliage
Late October Early November	Yamaguchi	CHOMONKYO	Chononkyo Gorge (one hour from Yamaguchi station)
		In Central Honshu	
All of October	Tochigi	FUKUWATA	Shiobara Spa
Mid-October Mid-November	Tochigi	NIKKO (area)	Daiya River, a long road to Lake Chuzenji, where autumn colors are especially abundant and brilliant
Mid-October Early November	Tochigi	KINUGAWA & KAWAJI SPAS	Two hours from Asakusa station, Tokyo
Mid-October Early November	Gumma	IKAO SPA	
Mid-October Early November	Gumma	KARUIZAWA (near)	Usui Pass (three hours from Tokyo)
Late October Mid-November	Tokyo	TOKYO (western area, accessible by cable car)	Mount Bushu-Mitake
Late October Mid-November	Kanagawa	LAKE SAGAMI	
Late October Mid-November	Kanagawa	HAKONE SPA	
Latter half of October	Yamanashi	FUJI-FIVE LAKES AREA	
		In Northern Honshu	
All of October	Border between Akita and Aomori	LAKE TOWADA	

Chrysanthemums are cultivated not in gardens but in pots. They are carefully taken to covered stands or chrysanthemum shows, where subtleties of form and color can be admired by all (above). The Japanese favor fantastic and bizarre forms, which reflect the many centuries of care devoted to these ornamentals (below).

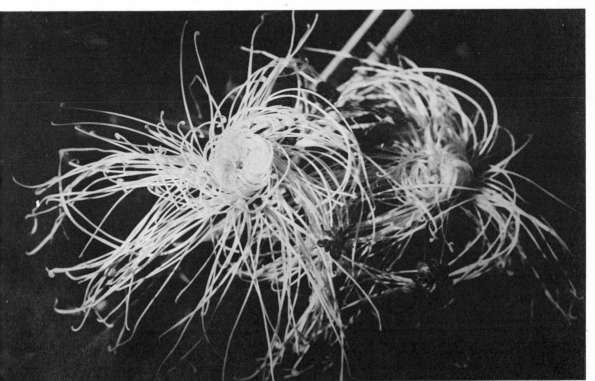

Season	Prefecture	Place	Location
Mid-October Late November	Miyagi	SENDAI (area)	Futakuchi Valley, along Natori River
All of October	Fukushima	ASAHI NATIONAL PARK	Bandai Plateau

In Hokkaido

Season	Prefecture	Place	Location
Early October		NOBORI-BETSU	Momiji-dani (Maple Valley). Mist and scarlet maples offer a memorable sight

Festivals with a Seasonal Touch

CHRYSANTHEMUM-VIEWING

The chrysanthemum (*kiku*), a flower that has been cultivated in Japan for fifteen hundred years, is used as the crest of the imperial family. Skillful Japanese horticulturists have developed varieties with almost unbelievable diversity of form and color. Gardeners delight in training the plants into imaginative cascades and other shapes, including life-size dolls made of chrysanthemum flowers and representing legendary heroes and heroines, an art unknown elsewhere. Visitors who expect to find chrysanthemums in nearly every Japanese garden at this season of the year will meet with disappointment. These flowers are usually planted in pots and must be sought out in selective displays in hothouses, hotel lobbies, railroad stations, stores, or gardens where the potted plants have been brought into gardens and placed among the permanent shrubs as a way of displaying them.

WHERE TO SEE CHRYSANTHEMUM DISPLAYS

Season	Prefecture	Place	Location

In Central Honshu

Season	Prefecture	Place	Location
Early half of November	Tokyo	TOKYO	Hibiya Park
Early half of November	Tokyo	TOKYO	Shinjuku Gyoen (Shinjuku Ward, Shinjuku Center Gardens, near outer garden of Meiji Shrine)
Late September Late November	Tokyo	TOKYO	Doll show at Tamagawa-en Recreation Park
October 20– November 30	Ibaraki	KASAMA	Doll show at Inari Shrine

In Western Honshu

Season	Prefecture	Place	Location
Late September Late November	Nara	NARA	Doll show at Ayamuki Park
October 1– November 30	Osaka	OSAKA	Doll show at Hirakata Recreation Park
October 10– November 20	Fukui	TAKEFU	Fine chrysanthemum doll show, best about November 3

(See also Chapter 15: CALENDAR OF JAPAN'S FESTIVAL YEAR.)

Uji's festival is a community affair; the orange-draped *mikoshi* (above), decorated with large bronze bells and topped by a phoenix, rests on its cart awaiting the bearers who will return it to the shrine. The festival features little ones also (below), who bear or help with their own diminutive *mikoshi*.

A master of ceremonies tattooed in rose and blue opens Osaka's Tenjin Festival (above).
Six men in peaked caps beat a monotonous thunder on a huge cart-borne drum (below).

Osaka's Tenjin Festival mixes reverence with hilarity. The priests bring with them an ethereal piping sound created by instruments such as the *sho,* an upright group of bamboo tubes that is a sort of elegant mouth organ, accompanied by beats on the *o-tsuzumi,* or hand drum (above). The mad shaking of manes and swirling of fabrics of the lion dance are a festive inheritance from China (below).

The Japanese fondness for turning a useful article into a ceremonial one is shown by the elaborate umbrella. The pattern of six disks on the side represents a cherry blossom, a symbol seen throughout the Tenjin Festival (left). Riding in a rikshaw, swathed in white silk, wearing a peculiar gauze cap, and shaded by a parasol, a geisha of ancient Japan is represented in the parade (right).

Eight men in orange drapery and straw sandals bear the curtained palanquin in the Aoi Festival (above). The flower-decked umbrella mingles gaiety with pomp (below).

Days of preparation precede the "launching" of a gigantic *hoko* float in the Gion parade. Workers tend it from a bridge that leads from the second story of a nearby building to the balcony of the float (left). Drawn by dozens of men who strain at two long ropes, the enormous *hoko* move ponderously through Kyoto's streets (right).

Cherry blossoms are a synonym for the arrival of spring in Japan. Little wonder that the Japanese, over the centuries, have developed varieties whose petals, white with nuances of pink, form fragrant clouds everywhere.

Purple sprays of wisteria mean midspring (right); they grace landscape gardens and homes. Later in spring, azaleas carpet the mountains and fill the forests with yellow, rose, orange, and lavender tones. On Mount Aso, a particularly fine display can be seen (left).

CALENDAR OF JAPAN'S FESTIVAL YEAR

Chapter 15–CALENDAR OF JAPAN'S FESTIVAL YEAR

January 1

NEW YEAR'S DAY (*Ganjitsu*). National Holiday

SHIHOHAI or Four Directions Worship

One of the four special holidays observed by the emperor. He worships in the direction of heaven, earth, mountains, and stars, this to ensure peace for the country and good crops. The custom has been observed since 590 A.D.

KAMAKURA MATSURI

At KAMAKURA, Tsurugaoka Hachiman Shrine. Kanagawa Prefecture.

Portable *mikoshi* are carried through the streets in this annual event. There is also target-shooting by horsemen attired as warriors of the Kamakura period.

OKERA MAIRI

At KYOTO, Yasaka Shrine. Kyoto Prefecture.

Held at daybreak on New Year's Day. A large number of worshipers visit the shrine seeking to bring home some of the sacred fire kindled by the priests, this to be used in cooking the first meal of the year, a custom believed to ward off illness during the year ahead.

January 1

NAGATA MATSURI

At KOBE, Nagata Shrine. Hyogo Prefecture.

Dedicated to Koto-Shironushi-no-Mikoto, ancient Shinto deity, worshiped as a promoter of good fortune and prosperity in trade. Crowds attend event at shrine on this day.

January 1–3

NEW YEAR'S HOLIDAYS

Observed throughout the country. Some rural areas have annual New Year's festivities according to the former lunar calendar, about a month later. (See also Chapter 12.)

January 1–14

SHUSHO-E MATSURI
At OSAKA, Shitennoji Shrine. Osaka Prefecture.

Held to pray for peace and an ample harvest. On the last day of the rituals, a very popular function, *Doyadoya*, is performed in which scantily-clad people scramble for a talisman believed to ward off evil.

January 3

GENSHI-SAI or First Beginning Ceremony

Held at *Kashikodokoro* (sanctuary of the Imperial Palace) as well as at local shrines; first held in 1870. Offerings are made at these sanctuaries when the princes and princesses and high courtiers are seated in their respective seats; the emperor appears and offers a sprig of sacred *sakaki* tree, reads the imperial proclamation before the gods, celestial, territorial, and imperial ancestors. This is one of the four great holidays observed by the emperor and his family.

January 3

TAMASESERI
At FUKUOKA, Hakozaki Shrine. Fukuoka Prefecture.

A priest in ceremonial dress throws a wooden ball that has been dipped in the sea. Stout-bodied youths, formed into two contesting teams, fight for the ball, and the winners offer the ball to the deity enshrined in the Hakozaki Shrine.

January 5

FIRST EBISU MATSURI
At NARA, Ebisu Shrine. Nara Prefecture.

Ebisu, one of the "seven deities of good fortune" so revered by merchants (and fishermen), is honored on this day. Approach to the shrine is lined with booths selling "luck-bringer" charms such as a figure of Ebisu and other items symbolizing wealth and good fortune. In western Japan, some of the Ebisu shrines hold their Toka Ebisu festivals on January 10: Kyoto at Kenninji Temple; Osaka at Imamiya Ebisu Shrine and Nishinomiya (between Kobe and Osaka).

January 5

SUITENGU MATSURI
At TOKYO, Suitengu Shrine. Tokyo Prefecture.

First festival of the year here. People visit the shrine to pray and buy charms to ensure their happiness in the new year.

January 6

DEZOME-SHIKI

At TOKYO, Meiji Shrine outer garden, or Hibiya Park. Tokyo Prefecture.

> Agile firemen perform acrobatics on top of tall bamboo ladders. A special feature of the capital since the Edo period; to show agility of Edo firemen when confronted with danger. Event unique and attracts much attention.

January 6

TOSHI-KOSHI MATSURI

At ITSUKUSHIMA (Island), Miyajima. Hiroshima Prefecture.

> Festival bidding the old year out and welcoming the new year in.

January 6–7

SHORINZAN DARUMA-ICHI

At TAKASAKI. Gumma Prefecture.

> Papier-mâché *daruma* tumbling dolls are sold at this season at doll markets here. They are a symbol of strong will and stubbornness as well as happiness. It is the custom to buy them with unpainted eyes, make a wish and paint in one eye, and when the wish is granted, paint in the other eye. Farmers make these dolls as an avocation. After the festival, people go to neighboring prefectures to sell the dolls during the winter months.

January 7

YANAIZU HADAKAMAIRI

At YANAIZU. Fukushima Prefecture.

> Temple priests assemble to pray for peace, intellect, and good harvests, Good-luck charms for health and safety are given to attendants at the ceremony. The name of the festival, which means "naked visit," refers to an old legend about men who, despite the winter weather, slew a dragon, thus putting an end to an epidemic and to a former ritual in which naked people used to run up one hundred stairs, climb up ropes, and throw down charms to the visitors.

January 7

NANAKUSA or Seven Herbs Festival

> One of the five traditional festivals celebrated throughout the country. All New Year's decorations within and outside the house are taken down. A rice gruel seasoned with seven herbs (shepherd's-purse, chickweed, *seri* or parsley, cottonweed or *gogyo*, *hiro* or radish, *hotoke-no-za* and *aona* or *Brassica chinensis*, although the exact contents of the gruel may vary somewhat) is served on this day.

January 7

ONISUBE USOKAE or Bullfinch Exchange

At FUKUOKA, Dazaifu Shrine. Fukuoka Prefecture.

Prior to a demon-chasing ceremony on the grounds of the shrine, people pass gold-decorated and undecorated bullfinches from hand to hand while sitting around the dim light of bonfires; everyone tries to end up with one of the good-luck golden bullfinches. Sometimes, marked and unmarked balls are used; the former signify good luck. As they play, participants keep saying, "Let's exchange!" The silent meaning is that they wish to exchange lies for sincerity (the marked balls).

January 8

MORIYAMA OKONAI MATSURI

At NOSU, Katsube Shrine. Shiga Prefecture.

Okonai means deeds, but the reason for so-naming this *matsuri* is obscure. There are twenty-five torch fires lighted after six o'clock in the evening, which burn with unusual brilliance and beauty.

January 9–16

HO-ONKO

At KYOTO, Nishi Honganji Temple. Kyoto Prefecture.

Annual service for the founder of the Jodo-Shinshu sect of Buddhism (Shinran), which has over nine thousand temples and more than six million adherents.

January 11–15

TA-UCHI (Rice-Field Work) or TA-ASOBI (Rice-Field Play)

New Year's rites still observed by farmers and rural people in many parts of the country. This old custom is observed to pray that the coming rice crop will be good. In many regions, villagers gather at the local shrine on some morning during the festival period and, after making a sacred rice paddy on the shrine grounds, go through solemn rites of planting and harvesting rice. This make-believe cultivation pageant is believed to ensure their good harvests. In other areas, the rite is performed by individual families and is done in a sacred plot marked for the purpose, and the family goes through the rites of planting and harvesting rice. In mountainous areas, the rites are even performed in the snow; pine needles are placed upright in the snow to represent rice seedlings. (See also Chapter 13: RICE AND OTHER FOOD FESTIVALS.)

January 13

ITABASHI SUWA JINJA TA-ASOBI

At TOKYO, Itabashi-ku, Suwa Shrine. Tokyo Prefecture.

The festival originated with an attempt on the part of the people to please the god of the paddy field (*ta-no-kami*) and in return expect a good harvest. After songs and refreshments, people have a *mikoshi* parade and special floats. An area is set aside where rice-planting dances, "weeding" dances, a "chasing away the bird" rite and dances representing the various stages in rice culture are given. One unusual dance represents fertility. At the end of the event, a big bonfire is lighted and the function is brought to an end with the beating of huge drums.

January 14

YUKI MATSURI or Snow Festival

At CHINO. Nagano Prefecture.

For several days before the festival officially opens, special purification rites are held, but the main festival begins on January 14 with a procession from the temple and through the snow to the main shrine. Dancing of various kinds, including a lion dance, and singing, a drum corps, music of flutes, and shouting, take place on the way to the shrine. Men carry rattles; boys carry drums but do not play them. Rites are performed and an offering is made as a supplication for spring fertility after winter barrenness. The climax of the festival occurs about midnight when a large pine tree bonfire is lighted and supposedly gods appear in the flames.

January 14

DONDOYAKI MATSURI

At SENDAI, Osaki Hachiman Shrine. Miyagi Prefecture.

On this night, pine tree boughs, straw-rope festoons, and New Year's decorations are brought from many homes in the city to the grounds of the shrine where a great bonfire is made—an event that attracts a large and merry crowd.

January 14

SNOW FESTIVAL

At TOKAMACHI. Niigata Prefecture.

Children build little igloo-like snow huts in which they sit and sing songs and have special food treats—a relic of ancient purification rites. Adults parade through the village with huge, colorful banners; farmers sell the products of their winter's work such as: straw raincoats, buckets, winnows, snowshoes.

January 14–15

KAPPA-KAPPA MATSURI
At KUROISHI. Aomori Prefecture.

A festival in which young men go from house to house carrying good-luck straw bags, and children carry dolls made of paper called *kappa-kappa;* they pray for good luck at each home visited.

January 15

SEIJIN-NO-HI or Adults' Day. National Holiday

Young men and women who have come of age are entertained by their parents, for they have achieved adulthood and an age at which they can vote and become full-fledged citizens. Programs are held in cities.

January 15

CHAKKIRAKO
At MIURA, Kainan Temple. Kanagawa Prefecture.

Dances are given by groups of young people of the fishing village; there are no instruments but they dance in time to their singing. Rhythm is made by bamboo sticks, such sounds being called *chakkirako.*

January 15

MATSUNOYAMA KAMIYAKI SUMINURI MATSURI
At MATSUNOYAMA. Niigata Prefecture.

An area is set aside in which to burn New Year's decorations. After burning takes place, snowy mud is added to the ashes and the mixture put on the participants' faces. They parade down the street afterward until they reach the appointed place, and they pause to pray to *Yakusi-sama,* god of medicine and healing, for health and safety for the coming year. The title of the *matsuri* relates to a god (*kami*) and burn (*yaki*) and black ink (*suminuri*).

January 15

TSURUGA TSUNAHIKI MATSURI or Tug-of-War Festival
At TSURUGA. Fukui Prefecture.

One of the chief ports of Japan, historically famous as the port from which communications were maintained with Korea from ancient times. The festival concerns *Ebisu,* god of luck for fishermen and merchants, and also *Daikoku,* god of wealth and good fortune. In the afternoon, the participants disguise themselves with masks and costumes representing the two gods and parade through the city. Later they participate in a tug of war, with the fishermen (representing *Ebisu*) on one side and the farmers (representing *Daikoku*) on the other end of the long rope. If the fishermen win, there will be good fishing; if the farmers win, they can be assured of a good harvest.

120

January 15

WAKAKUSAYAMAYAKI or Mount Wakakusa Dead-Grass-Burning Event
At NARA. Nara Prefecture.

A special celebration is held in Nara on Wakakusayama Hill in the evening—a thrilling sight. The festival reminds Nara people of the historic burning of the hill ten centuries before, which marked the amicable dispute concerning the boundaries of two major temples in Nara. There are fireworks and other entertainment in connection with the event.

January 15–17

ATAMI UME MATSURI or Apricot Festival
At ATAMI. Shizuoka Prefecture.

The early-blooming variety of apricot blooms from the end of December to approximately the middle of January, and the people take advantage of this by having a festival. During this time there are such events as caged-nightingale singing contests and photography contests.

January 18

SAMEGAWA JINJA MISOGI or Purification Ceremony
At KIKONAI. Samegawa Shrine. Hokkaido.

The festival, begun in the Tempo era (1830–1847), consists of a purification ceremony whereby four unmarried young men carry a sacred *mikoshi* (with deified spirit) into the ocean where it is ceremoniously cleansed in the water.

January 18

HATSU-U-MODE
At TOKYO, Kameido Tenjin Shrine. Tokyo Prefecture.

The date of the festival is somewhat variable. The event is one of the most colorful in the capital city.

January 21

HATSU-DAISHI or First Daishi Day
At KAWASAKI, Daishi Temple. Kanagawa Prefecture.

Many Daishi temples—dedicated to Kobo-Daishi (774–835), first exponent of Shingon doctrines in Japan—have special rites on this day, notably this one in Kawasaki (between Tokyo and Yokohama).

January 25

TENJIN MATSURI
At OSAKA, Kitano Shrine. Kyoto Prefecture.

Popularly known as *Kitano Tenjin,* dedicated to Sugawara Michizane, who was deified under the name of Tenjin. This is the first Tenjin Festival of the year at the Kitano Shrine.

February 1–2

KUROKAWA NO

At KUSHIBIKI. Yamagata Prefecture.

On February 1, villagers go to the home of the elder member of the community, who has brought an object of worship from the shrine to his home. Throughout the night, the villagers present five or six No plays. On February 2, they present the No plays (there are 540 from which to choose), in the compound of the Kasuga Shrine. When not too busy on farms, these villagers prepare themselves for this annual presentation of No plays.

February 1–3 (Variable)

SETSUBUN or Bean-Throwing Ceremony

This day (February 1) marks the "parting of the seasons"—the end of winter and the beginning of spring—and the Japanese people observe the time-honored ceremony of bean-throwing or *mame-make* on the eve of the new season. Thousands of people of Tokyo, for instance, make pilgrimages to prominent temples and shrines to offer prayers and witness the bean-throwing spectacle. At the noted temples and shrines, important people are chosen to do the bean-throwing, it being considered an honor to do so. The primary function of the day, however, is carried on in many homes, for on that night may be heard: "Oni wa soto. Fuku wa uchi," meaning "Go out, devils! Come in, good luck!" Roasted beans are thrown at door entrances and into rooms of houses, especially into dark corners where devils might lurk. One of the largest such ceremonies of this kind is held at 4 P.M. at Narita, Shinshoji Temple, Chiba Prefecture; thousands flock to see it. The Horyuji Temple at Nara features costumed demons who are figuratively chased away by gods. In Kyoto, on February 2 and 3, there is a demon-exorcising festival called *Tsuinashiki* (also at Mibu Shrine and Kurama Temple). At Kawasaki, Daishi Temple, Kanagawa Prefecture, there is another notable ceremony of this kind.

February 1–8

OWASE YAYA MATSURI or "Shouting" Festival

At OWASE, Owase Shrine. Mie Prefecture.

This is one of the "quarrel festivals" in which *mikoshi* carried by lively young men meet and collide with each other as they parade down the street. When they meet, one group's members yell "Yaya Yaya," hence the name of the event. Houses along the line of the parade have to install protective fences. During the period of the festivals, several special events take place, including dances. On the last night a ceremony is held at the Owase Shrine to determine the participants for the event the following year.

Japan's bean-throwing ceremony symbolizes ritual purification, but despite the seriousness of the theme, large crowds gather in hopes of catching beans, which can be used in their homes to cast devils out of dark corners. (February 1–3.)

February 2

GOHANSHIKI or Rice Ceremony

At NIKKO, Rinnoji Temple. Tochigi Prefecture.

At the end of the ceremony, toy vegetables, fruits, and sweets are given to the assembled crowd. In feudal times, the daimyo who visited Nikko to pay homage to the Toshogu Shrine were required to eat huge bowls of rice, a test of a daimyo's loyalty to the deity of the shrine. The priests also have a ceremony of lighting the holy fire, and then do dances to a song accompaniment. (See also Chapter 13: RICE AND OTHER FOOD FESTIVALS.)

123

February 3

HORAIJI DENGAKU MATSURI

At HORAI, Horaiji Temple. Aichi Prefecture.

Very famous temple of the Shingon sect. Legend has it that demons guarded the nearby mountains and gave their lives to protect them. At this festival, costumes of red, black, and blue represent these demons. A team of men *dengaku* dancers go to the stage of the temple, ring a bell, and offer sake to the enshrined body; then they present ten to twelve kinds of dances. At the end, a huge rice cake is offered at the shrine altar. In the afternoon, the *dengaku* dances are resumed.

February 3 or 4

MANDO-E or Lantern-Lighting Ceremony

At NARA, Kasuga Shrine. Nara Prefecture.

All three thousand lanterns of the Kasuga Shrine are lighted to welcome the spring season. Also, torches are kindled in the precinct grounds. The sight of the illumination viewed in the dark woods is an exciting one. (See also August 15.)

At the Kasuga Shrine of Nara, hundreds of lanterns are lighted; this eerie spectacle lights the way for visits from departed spirits. (February 3 or 4.)

February 4 (Variable)

ONIOI-SHIKI or Demon-Driving Ceremony

At NARA, Kofukuji Temple. Nara Prefecture.

At KOBE, Nagata Shrine. Hyogo Prefecture.

After a religious rite in early evening, men dressed as demons run nosily into the temple or shrine grounds and mingle with the onlookers. Soon thereafter, disguised Buddhist priests race in and drive the demons down the streets, through the shopping areas, and back to the temple. A bean-throwing ceremony follows such as the one described under February 1–3.

February 5-7

YUKI MATSURI or Snow Festival

At SAPPORO. Hokkaido.

Largest festival held in Hokkaido. Molded snow images are shown on the main street and festivals are held. There is a costumed dress parade and skating contests. About this time of year, similar festivals are held at Tokamachi, Niigata Prefecture, and several other cities in northern Honshu. Radio and television studios broadcast the events.

At Sapporo's Snow Festival, or Yuki Matsuri, the Japanese sense of craft is seen in the careful sculpturing of massive snow figures in Greek style. (February 5–7.)

February 12

HATUSU-UMA MATSURI or First Horse Day (Lunar) Festival
At KYOTO, Inari Shrine (and other shrines throughout the country). Kyoto Prefecture.

This day is especially dedicated to the god of crops. Thousands of worshipers and visitors flock to the Inari shrine here and elsewhere on this day. Effigies of foxes are seen along roads, placed there because they represent the god's messengers. As one approaches the shrine, the noise is almost deafening, dominated by the sounds of wooden clogs on the flagstones, metal bells and gongs, and muted voices in prayer. Huge banners bearing the name of the Inari deity are planted around a tall red *torii*, and drums are beaten in turn by spectators. All Inari shrines are well-known, celebrated in song and story since feudal days. *Hatusu-uma* celebrations are said to have originated in the ninth century.

February 14–15

SHIMMEISHA ONI MATSURI
At TOYOHASHI, Shimmeisha Shrine. Aichi Prefecture.

In this old castle town there is an annual traditional *dengaku* dance festival. On the fifteenth, children with crowns containing the sun and moon present the "sunrise" sacred *kagura* dance. The main event takes place on an octagonal stone stage with the presentation of several kinds of sacred dances, one of which is given by a "red demon" who has an imaginary fight with a costumed goblin.

February 15

OMAGARI TSUNAHIKI TORIOI
At OMAGARI, Suwa Shrine. Akita Prefecture.

A ceremony to pray for good harvests and prosperity in business. A *torioi* or bird-chasing dance is performed by Shinto priests; they throw good-luck wands to spectators, who scramble to secure them. In the evening a long, heavy rope is paraded through the streets to the accompaniment of music. On the road near the shrine, villagers are divided into an upper and a lower team and engage in a tug of war (*tsunahiki*). If the upper team wins, the price of rice will be good that season; if the lower team wins, the price of rice will be lower—a sort of divination ceremony.

February 15–17

KAMAKURA MATSURI

At YOKOTE. Akita Prefecture.

Children make igloos of snow and stay in them overnight. A little altar is made to the deity of water. By candlelight, the children serve sweet sake to passing neighbors, who in turn give the children a small amount of money or fruit. Also, there is a contest in Yokote to determine the best snow sculpture made. Similar festival at Tokomachi, Niigata Prefecture, on January 14.

In northern Japan's Kamakura Matsuri, snow huts serve as cheery candlelit centers in the cold, dark night. As with any Japanese home or temple, shoes (often straw ones in this part of Japan) are left at the doorway. (February 15–17.)

February 15–March 31

NINGYODERA NINGYOTEN

At KYOTO, Hokyoji Temple. Kyoto Prefecture.

This is an exhibition of dolls (*ningyo*) through the eras of Japan's history; also an exhibit of dolls once belonging to court ladies.

The carnival spirit prevails at a winter festival at Tokamachi, Niigata Prefecture, where snow arches and booths form streetside markets. (February 15–17.)

February 15–17 (Variable)

TOKAMACHI YUKI MATSURI

At TOKAMACHI. Niigata Prefecture.

Fifteen years ago this festival began to attract tourists. A fashion and talent show is presented on a snow stage. In addition to a costumed parade, other features include a photography contest, skiing contest, and exhibit of snow sculptures. It is the largest festival held in this prefecture.

February 17

BONDEN MATSURI

At YOKOTE. Akita Prefecture.

Following the Kamakura Festival (see above, February 15–17), about fifty people carry long poles at the top of which is a bamboo basket on each one, covered with brightly colored cloth and streamers (called *bonden*). As they parade with them through the snow, they sing songs and are accompanied by flutists until they reach their destination at the local shrine, where the *bonden* are given as an offering.

The Bonden Festival at Yokote, Akita Prefecture, features weird, balloonlike standards. (February 17.)

February 17–20

EMBURI

At HACHINOHE. Aomori Prefecture.

To pray for a rich harvest, grouped villagers dance along a trail up Mount Choya in a gala procession to the accompaniment of drums, flutes, and other instruments. There are also dancers and a special celebration in the city.

Third Saturday in February (Approximately)

EYO MATSURI

At SAIDAIJI, Saidaiji Temple. Okayama Prefecture.

In the ancient Kannon Temple here, there is a very exciting and curious festival. After several drum parades in the evening, a large number of stout-bodied youths file into the temple grounds about eleven o'clock uttering peculiar sounds, and supposedly pray for the divine mercy of Kannon. The priest throws a pair of sacred wands into the crowd and a cyclonic encounter ensues. Any young man who is able to pick up and keep one of these *shingi* wands is promised a life of luxury and happiness.

MIZUSAWA HIBUSE MATSURI

At MIZUSAWA, Hidaka Shrine. Iwate Prefecture.

The festival has a history of three hundred years and is held as an occasion to pray for the prevention of disastrous fires and for good rice harvests. Representatives of each area go to Hidaka Shrine to secure good-luck charms; return with them to the starting place for a parade. There is a drum float upon which are young boys and a float upon which girls ride and who are dressed in the formal dress of ancient days. Attracts many thousands, as it is considered one of the outstanding Japanese festivals.

February 24–25

KATSUYAMA SAGICHO

At KATSUYAMA. Fukui Prefecture.

A kind of fire festival with Chinese influence. Twelve two-storied stages are constructed, decorated with red-and-white striped cloth and many lanterns, statuettes, and pine trees (symbol of deity). Samisens, flutes, and drums provide the musical background. At ten o'clock on the twenty-fifth, the pine decorations (*sagicho*) are put in a pile on the banks of the river and a huge bonfire made of them.

February 25

TENJIN MATSURI

The Tenjin shrines in the country celebrate this festival day in memory of Sugawara Michizane (845–903), famous scholar-statesman, who was deified under the name Tenjin. People all over Japan go to the Tenjin shrines, make rice offerings as well as branches of the Japanese apricot tree, a tree much loved. by Michizane. See also Chapter 14 for places to see famous apricot trees and apricot groves in bloom during this month and through early April.

March 1

Beginning of March

YUZAWA SKI CARNIVAL

At MINAMI, Uonuma-gun. Niigata Prefecture.

A snow castle is built and lighted at night; there is also a fireworks display; and over one hundred people on skis engage in a torchlight parade. Also, a kimono show may be seen.

March 3

URASA BISHAMONDO OSHIAI MATSURI

At YAMATO, Shinkoji Temple. Niigata Prefecture.

This festival was originated for the purpose of praying for a good harvest year. Nearby is a waterfall, and at six-thirty in the evening, many half-clothed young men brave the still cold weather, crack the ice of the frozen waterfall, scoop up the water underneath, and bring it to the Bishamondo (a building in the temple compound). A strange part of the ceremony involves "pushing and pulling" (*oshiai*) in an effort to get upon a high shelf containing a Buddha statue. Those who are able to get to the shelf pray for a rich harvest during the coming season.

March 3

HINA MATSURI or Dolls' Day

Observed throughout Japan. Sometimes called *Momo-no-sekku* or Peach-Blossom Festival or Girls' Day. (See Chapter 10 for full description of the event.)

First Saturday in March

BIWAKO KOSUIBIRAKI

At OTSU (southern end of Lake Biwa). Shiga Prefecture.

This festival, begun only a few years ago, celebrates the opening season at Lake Biwa. Prior to the beginning of the sight-seeing tours of the season, a boat festival takes place in which there are over one hundred boats of many sizes and with varied decorations. Upon these boats over one thousand school children from Kobe, Osaka, and surrounding areas ride in a circular parade around the lake. Brass bands play; greetings are given by the drum major; important people are introduced and given bouquets. At a given time, flowers are thrown into the lake; one group of boats go north, another south, and the lake is declared open for the season.

March 12

O-MIZUTORI MATSURI or Water-Drawing Ceremony

At NARA, Todaiji Temple. Nara Prefecture.

This festival is the most famous one of this temple and actually is scheduled from March 1 to 15, but the main feature is on this day. On the evening of the twelfth, thousands of people witness the lighting of huge torches and the ancient ceremony of drawing the holy water from the Wakasa Well below February Hall by the temple. The atmosphere of the weird midnight rituals is enhanced by the wailing sound of large shell-horns blown by priests in white robes. The function is said to have been observed annually for about twelve centuries. When the torch-bearers reach the hill, they stand around the hall and swing the torches to produce showers of sparks. The scene is an amazing one and the hall appears to be floating in flames. As cinders are believed to be charms against evil spirits, spectators make frantic efforts to get them. This continues until midnight when the supreme moment comes for the observance of drawing the holy water from the celebrated Wakasa Well, the structure around it being festooned with rice-straw ropes (*shimenawa*) to which are attached zigzag white papers, symbolic of sacredness. Branches of the sacred tree are brought from Mount Kasuga for decorations. As the water is drawn there is an atmosphere of solemnity. Some of the water is given to people to take home, as it is believed to have some power of healing; some is put into airtight jars and placed on the altar of Kannon, goddess of mercy. There is an old Japanese saying that there will be no warm weather until after *O-Mizutori*, that this time marks the break between the seasons.

March 13

KASUGA MATSURI
At NARA, Kasuga Shrine. Nara Prefecture.

This shrine, one of the oldest and most picturesque in Japan, holds this annual festival with elaborate ceremonies, reproducing scenes reminiscent of other days when the shrine was in its glory. One of the features of the occasion is a procession that morning through Nara Park with Buddhist and Shinto priests dressed in representative ancient court costumes. Another feature is the sacred dance performance of Shinto maidens of the shrine.

March 13–15

OMIHACHIMAN SAGICHO MATSURI
At OMIHACHIMAN, Hachimangu Shrine. Shiga Prefecture.

A large pyramid is made of straw handles. At the center is placed a ninety-foot pole which is decorated with streamers, fans, etc. This and others like it are carried through the town like a *mikoshi* accompanied by people wearing red-lacquered wooden clogs and who keep time with wooden clappers as they walk in the parade. After dark, the *sagicho* (decorations) are taken to the shrine where each in turn is set afire.

March 15

HIMENOMIYA HONEN MATSURI or Good Harvest Festival
At INUYAMA, Ogata Shrine. Aichi Prefecture.

Here by the Kiso River stands a well-known castle on a hill from which there is a superb view of the rapids below. The cormorant fishing season from June to October attracts many. On this day there is an unusual parade the main interest of which centers around a huge clam-shell float that opens and closes slowly. It opens to reveal a charming girl inside who throws little rice cakes to spectators. Apparently the *mikoshi* with the clam shell represents fertility; the girl, motherhood; and the rice cakes, progeny.

March 15

NIHAN-E or Anniversary of Buddha's Death
At KYOTO, Seiryoji and Tofukuji Temples. Kyoto Prefecture.

Buddhist services are held in memory of Buddha, who died or entered Nirvana on this day. Tofukuji Temple displays a picture showing Buddha's entry into Nirvana. When the sacred torches are lighted in the temples, the public is permitted in.

March 21

SHUMBUN-NO-HI or Vernal Equinox Day. National Holiday

The week during which the vernal equinox occurs is called *higan,* which means "other shore" and comes from the idea, according to Buddhist belief, that there is a river marking the division between this earthly world and the future one. Only when one crosses the river, fighting strong currents of temptation, to the "other shore" does he gain enlightenment. The observance of the season was started by Prince Shotoku in the seventh century. It was made a national holiday in the Meiji era in view of its general religious significance to the people. The visit to the family cemetery is a happy event in some districts; the people have a merry time there with food and sake. Common *higan* food (no meat) is *o-hagi* or soft rice balls covered with sweetened bean paste. *Sushi,* or vinegared rice with vegetables, is also made in some homes and offered to ancestors and neighbors. It is a holiday set aside to honor nature and show respect for growing things also. (See September 20 – Autumn Equinox.)

March 23

SHUNKI-KOREI-SAN or Spring Imperial Spirit Festival

The emperor pays special respect to his imperial ancestors; the custom was originated by the first emperor, Jimmu, in 660 B.C. when he ascended the throne and reported the event to his ancestors.

Variable During Month of March

SHISHI ODORI or Deer Dance
At HANANOMAKI. Iwate Prefecture.

Eight men wear antlered deer masks and re-create three peculiar but fascinating dances: the sunlight, moonlight, and starlight dance; a slow formal dance; and a dance representing the life of a deer. This kind of dancing is unique to this particular area and is given during this month at the request of visitors.

133

The *Shishi Odori* (Deer Dance) of Hananomaki, Iwate Prefecture, is unlike any other festival found in Japan. (Variable during the month of March.)

March–April

CHERRY-BLOSSOM-VIEWING FESTIVALS

Throughout the country. (See also Chapter 14 for best places to see cherry blossoms.)

April 1–10

MIYAKO ODORI or Capital Dance

At KYOTO, Kaburenjo Theater. Kyoto Prefecture.

The best available artists and musicians take part in these performances. The first scene, lantern-decorated, is especially beautiful, as are the geisha dances executed with a series of graceful posturings done to the accompaniment of samisens, flutes, and drums. Before each performance, those holding first- and second-class tickets may attend a tea ceremony at which tea is served to visitors.

April 1–14

ASHIBE ODORI

At osaka, Asahiza Theater. Osaka Prefecture.

Japanese folk dancers; cherry-blossom dances done by geisha girls.

April 1–25

AZUMA ODORI

At tokyo, Shimbashi Embujo Theater. Tokyo Prefecture.

Shimbashi geisha dancers perform in this theater during April.

April 3

KASHIHARA SHINSHIKISAI or Shinto Event

At kashihara, Kashihara Shrine. Nara Prefecture.

The Kashihara Shrine where this ceremony is held was built of timbers which were once part of the Imperial Palace in Kyoto. It was built in 1889, dedicated to the first emperor, Jimmu. This event is to console the deity of the shrine. No plays are presented by the famous Komparu No school, and thousands of people come to see the plays. There is a ceremony of "freeing doves" and other attractions.

April 3–5

KATORI OTAUE MATSURI or Rice Festival

At katori, Katori Shrine, Chiba Prefecture.

In the shrine compound here, as in so many others, there is a sacred paddy field. In this event (in which there are musicians), a person disguised as a god of storm, planting maidens, etc., circle around the rice paddy and act out the various stages involved in rice cultivation. (See also Chapter 13: Rice and Other Food Festivals.)

April 3–29

NAGASAKI TAKOAGE or Kite-Flying Event

At nagasaki. Nagasaki Prefecture.

It is believed that a Portuguese who was homesick drew a picture or map of his country and then made a kite from it, thus introducing the custom of kite-flying to Japan. The kites used at this event are usually diamond-shaped with an infinite variety of patterns and decorations on them. As in other such events, there is a contest (this is one of the most famous ones) in which participants try to cut loose the kites of their opponents by the use of glass bits or sharp objects on their kite strings.

135

April 5–7

ISE SHRINE KAGURA MATSURI

At ISE, Ise Shrine. Mie Prefecture.

If one is a devotee of No plays, this is the time and place to see them, as the very best No players from Japan are brought here for these performances. Besides the No plays, sacred *kagura* pantomime dances are performed, a notable one being a "Butterfly Dance," *kocho-no-mai*. (See also September 23–25.)

April 5–20

KITANO ODORI

At KYOTO, Kitano Kaikan Theater. Kyoto Prefecture.

Geisha dance performances. (See also November 1–15.)

April 6–7

DAIGO SAKURAKAI

At KYOTO, Daigoji Temple. Kyoto Prefecture.

Cherry dances performed by talented geishas. One scene portrays General Toyotomi Hideyoshi viewing cherry blossoms. A tea ceremony is held in connection with the performance.

April 7–14

TSURUGAOKA HACHIMAN (SHRINE) SPRING FESTIVAL

At KAMAKURA, Hachiman Shrine. Kanagawa Prefecture.

The festival at this season of the year is significant because Kamakura was the first seat of feudal government some seven centuries ago, and because the cherry blossoms have always been regarded as a symbol of gallant knighthood. With this setting, the function is properly called a spring cherry festival, and attracts hundreds of thousands of holiday-makers and visitors during the season. There are many events and many kinds of parades, something different every day of this week.

April 8

HANA MATSURI or Flower Festival

BUDDHA'S BIRTHDAY

The birthday of Gautama Buddha (Sakyamuni), founder of Buddhism, is observed in all Buddhist temples in Japan. (See Chapter 8 for full description.)

April 9

INARI MATSURI

At KYOTO, Inari Shrine. Kyoto Prefecture.

Another interesting festival at a famous shrine.

April 9–14

KADO KYOTEN

At KYOTO, Daimaru Department Store. Kyoto Prefecture.

For those interested in flower arrangement exhibitions, this is a noteworthy one to see, with thirty-four flower arrangement schools represented, and with two sections each having one hundred or more flower arrangements.

April 10

YASURAI MATSURI

At KYOTO, Imamiya Shrine. Kyoto Prefecture.

The origin of the festival dates back to the eighth century, when the people prayed before the god of the shrine asking for help in abating a serious epidemic. Several features of the festival are: a costumed parade representing court nobles and their retinues; a procession of men dressed as devils; and priests trotting along the streets chanting an old paddy-field song, "Yasurai" (meaning "Relax").

April 10

HIRANO SAKURA MATSURI

At KYOTO, Hirano Shrine. Kyoto Prefecture.

A costume parade that originated in the Heian era.

April 13

SHIRAHATAGU (SHRINE) MATSURI

At KAMAKURA. Kanagawa Prefecture.

Annual shrine festival.

April 13

ARASHIYAMA JUSANMAIRI or Thirteen-Pilgrims Event

At KYOTO, Horinji Temple. Kyoto Prefecture.

A pilgrimage of thirteen-year-old children for the purpose of being endowed with some of Kokuzo's wisdom. An image of Kokuzo, a Buddhist god of wisdom, is enshrined in the temple. The grounds have many fine cherry trees and command an excellent view of the surrounding country. The Horinji Temple is on an eminence south of Arashiyama.

April 13–15

ZOJOJI (TEMPLE) MATSURI

At TOKYO, Zojoji Temple, Shiba Park. Tokyo Prefecture.

Elaborate ceremonies to observe the death anniversary of St. Honen, founder of the Jodo sect of Buddhism. The occasion is the greatest event in the Jodo sect calendar and is marked by a large procession consisting of several hundred priests, laymen, and children dressed in costumes of former days.

Processions and services are held every afternoon for three days. A large group of firemen heads the procession chanting "Kiyari," their vocational song, to clear the way for the marchers. The group is followed by about thirty men dressed in blue *kamishimo*, ceremonial dress worn on official occasions; then by men each carrying a large red-lacquer tray mounted with offerings to St. Honen; and a file of about sixty priests of high rank in heavy brocade robes, chanting Buddhist sutras. As they march, they scatter red, green, white, and gold artificial lotus leaves.

April 13–16

NAGAHAMA YAMAKYOGEN

At NAGAHAMA, Hachiman Shrine. Shiga Prefecture.

This city, located on the east shore of Lake Biwa, is noted for its manufacture of fine silk crepes. General Toyotomi Hideyoshi's son gave money to the townspeople of Nagahama and they used it to build twelve festival floats (*yama*). As the silk industry grew and prospered, so grew the beauty of the floats, until today they are unusually ornate with their red, gold, and silver lacquer work and tapestries. On the thirteenth, the decoration of the floats is completed and lots drawn for their order in the parade. On the next day the *yamas* are taken to the shrine. On the fifteenth, children with long wooden swords (*tachi*) precede the floats down the street. Occasionally the *yama* stop and a short play (*kyogen*) is presented on the float. The event ends after a final lantern-lighting ceremony.

April 13–17

YAYOI MATSURI

At NIKKO, Futaarasan Shrine. Tochigi Prefecture.

This is one of the largest local festivals and the chief one of this shrine, being combined with festivals of its subsidiary shrines. On April 13, the portable shrines are fitted up; and on April 14, a *mikoshi* of the Takino-o Shrine, accompanied by priests and groups of men, women, musicians, and dancers, is carried from the Futaarasan Shrine along the main road. On the seventeenth, a ceremony is held in front of three portable shrines, then placed in the oratory. Afterward the shrines are carried in a grand procession to the Hongu Shrine where an ancient ceremony is performed before they are returned to the Futaarasan Shrine. Decorated *mikoshi* from fifteen sections of the city are part of the grand procession.

April 14

ANJIN MATSURI

At YOKOSUKA, Tsukayama Park, near Anjin station. Yamanashi Prefecture.

William Adams, an Englishman, served Shogun Tokugawa Ieyasu; taught Western gunnery, shipbuilding, navigation, mathematics, and other technical Western subjects. He married a Japanese, took the name of Miura

Anjin, and died at Hirado, near Nagasaki, at the age of fifty-six. Later, the ashes of Anjin and his wife were put in a tomb in Tsukayama Park, which is part of the estate given him by the shogun in return for his able services. When the cherry-blossom season is at its best, a memorial service is held in front of the tombs.

First or Second Saturday in April

SHENSHOKU MATSURI or Textile Festival

At KYOTO. Kyoto Prefecture.

The festival is held under the auspices of the Society of Weavers and Dyers of the city. The function is an expression to deities for the success given to industries through the year. Features of the festival include dance and song performances and a procession of young women dressed in beautiful brocade kimonos. A very interesting new Kyoto festival.

April 14–15

SANNO MATSURI

At TAKAYAMA, Hie Shrine. Gifu Prefecture.

Takayama is a small mountain town but it has an annual festival with twenty-three magnificent festival floats embellished with elaborate metalware, wood carvings, and tapestries of ancient workmanship. On the carefully planned floats are movable stages with mechanical figures.

April 15 to Late May

KAMOGAWA ODORI

At KYOTO, Ponto-cho Kiburenjo Theater. Kyoto Prefecture.

Spring dance festival; more modern in dancing, music, settings, etc., than Miyako Odori, which is more classical in character. Performances given twice a year (see October 5–28). Started in 1872. Tea ceremony demonstration and participation is part of the performance.

Mid-April

SAKURA MATSURI or Cherry Festival

At NARA. Nara Prefecture.

One of the most gorgeous festivals of its kind held in Nara. On the festival day there is a colorful procession of young girls and children who carry cherry blossoms in a parade through the main street. Shops vie with each other in displaying beautiful seasonal decorations.

April 15–28

KYO ODORI and KITANO ODORI

At KYOTO, Minamiza Theater, Kitano Kaikan Theater. Kyoto Prefecture.

Japanese dance and music festival. The Kyo Odori is presented at the Minamiza Theater; the Kitano Odori at the Kitano Kaikan Theater.

139

Highly-embellished floats surmounted by drums or miniature shrines take part in the Sanno Matsuri of Takayama, Gifu Prefecture. (April 14–15.)

April 15–16

IKUTA (SHRINE) MATSURI

At KOBE, Ikuta Shrine. Hyogo Prefecture.

The festival of this shrine is held with great ceremony to celebrate construction of the shrine.

April 16–17

TOSHOGU (SHRINE) MATSURI

At NAGOYA. Aichi Prefecture.

The festival held annually at this shrine is one of the largest held in Nagoya. On the sixteenth, dances are presented; on the seventeenth, a *mikoshi* parade.

April 16–18

ITSUKUSHIMA JINJA SHINNO

At ITSUKUSHIMA (Island), Itsukushima Shrine. Hiroshima Prefecture.

On this island (also known as Miyajima), the Kita and Okera schools of No present No plays on an outdoor stage that is historically famous.

April 16–23

BUNSUI OIRAN DOCHU or Courtesan Parade

At NISHIKANBARA. Niigata Prefecture.

A modern festival with such features as: April 16, opening of Bunsui Park; 17 and 18, sake-tasting event; 19, a flower festival; 20, Japanese dances by geisha girls; 22, dance and music presentations; and on the twenty-third (usually the third Sunday), there is a courtesan parade which is the main attraction. Many geishas are trained here in a special school. Girls are chosen for the parade not only for their beauty and physique, but they must be able to wear some of the gorgeous costumes, some of them so elaborately decorated (and worn one on top of another) that they may weigh fifty pounds or more.

April 17

MADARA KIJINSAI or Demon-God Event

At YAMATOMURA, Rakuhoji Temple. Ibaraki Prefecture.

Legend has it that once the fourteenth-century temple burned down, and Madara, the demon-god, gathered together many demons who reconstructed the temple in seven days; then he danced around a bonfire in celebration of their completed work and to wish the temple prosperity in the future. This festival is in appreciation of Madara and the demons; men disguise themselves as demons and ride their horses up 145 stairs. There are demon dances to add to the strange event. Since there are many cherry trees in bloom here at this season, spectators come to attend the festival and to enjoy the beauty of the cherry blossoms.

April 20

KURAMA HANAKUYO or Flower Memorial Service
At KYOTO, Kurama Temple. Kyoto Prefecture.

Attractions at this event include: tea ceremony, flower arrangement exhibits, a *chigo* (children's) parade, music and dancing.

April 21

SHUZENJI ONSEN YUKUMI MATSURI
At SHUZENJI. Shizuoka Prefecture.

Shuzenji (Spa) is noted for its hot springs, which are beneficial in gastric and skin diseases. It is one of the three most popular spas on the Izu Peninsula. It is believed that Priest Kobo-Daishi, first exponent of the Shingon sect of Buddhism, struck a rock in this area, causing water to gush out. In celebrating this festival, the priest Kobo is given special thanks and water is scooped out of the hot springs and offered to him. There are a costumed parade and a *chigo* parade also.

April 21

UBE (SHRINE) HARU MATSURI or Spring Festival
At IWAMI, Ube Shrine. Tottori Prefecture.

Longevity is the idea behind one of the main features of this festival, an unusual Lion Dance symbolic of the lion's ability to ward off epidemics and thus prolong life. Other features of the festival are: scores of armored warriors, huge *mikoshi* requiring as many as one hundred men to carry them, groups of men and women dancers.

April 21–25

YASUKUNI (SHRINE) MATSURI
At TOKYO, Yasakuni Shrine. Tokyo Prefecture.

The shrine on top of Kudan Hill in Chiyodaku, Tokyo, holds a spring festival for four days. The shrine is known as a military one; the object of worship here is the deified spirits of the Japanese soldiers who died in wars at home and abroad for their country. All visitors to the shrine are entertained with dances, stage plays, motion-picture shows, fireworks, etc. Scores of vases of flowers are arranged by well-known masters in the art and exhibited in the courtyard.

April 21–29

MIBU DAINEMBUTSU KYOGEN
At KYOTO, Mibu Temple. Kyoto Prefecture.

This event dates back to 1299. Buddhist farces or religious plays are performed entirely in pantomime with thirty characters who wear ancient wooden masks. Four or five *kyogen* are presented each day from one to five o'clock except on the last day, when the performances last until ten o'clock at night.

April 23–25

SENTEISAI MATSURI or Courtesan Festival
At SHIMONOSEKI. Yamaguchi Prefecture.

This festival dates back many years, to a time when court ladies became widows as a result of their husbands being lost in battle, and became courtesans. In sympathy for the court ladies, women in Shimonoseki don courtesan attire and participate in a festival commemorating them.

Calendar of Japan's Festival Year

The ladies of the Senteisai Festival of Shimonoseki, Yamaguchi Prefecture, commemorate the widows of an early day who became courtesans. (April 23–25.)

April 24–25

SHIOGAMA HANAMATSURI or Flower Festival
At SHIOGAMA, Shiogama Shrine. Miyagi Prefecture.

A large number of people carry a huge *mikoshi* up the 202 steps to the
shrine, located on a hill surrounded by gigantic cedar trees. Since the
enshrined deities are guardians of seamen, there are *yama* in the shape
of whales, large and small. Fireworks displays are also a feature of the
festival.

April 27–29

MINATO MATSURI or Port Festival
At NAGASAKI. Nagasaki Prefecture.

This festival is celebrated in commemoration of the opening of Nagasaki
in the sixteenth century as Japan's only foreign trade port. Highlights of
the festival are a fireworks display, folk song contest, and a costume parade.
On the twenty-seventh the Nagasaki fish market has a memorial service
for fish that have been caught, and there is a fireworks display in the
evening. The famous *Peiron* (boat race) takes place on the afternoon of
the last day of the festival.

April 29

KAMAKURA MATSURI
At KAMAKURA. Kanagawa Prefecture.

A historic parade with many costumed participants.

April 29

EMPEROR'S BIRTHDAY (*Tenno Tanjobi*). National Holiday

Fourth Sunday in April

SHINKOSAI or Rice-Offering Event
At KYOTO, Matsuno-o Shrine. Kyoto Prefecture.

A well-known rice-offering festival. Six sacred shrines are paraded through
the streets, presenting a spectacular sight.

Late April–Early May

AZALEA-VIEWING

See Chapter 14 for azalea-viewing areas.

144

May 1

TAKAOKA YAMA MATSURI

At TAKAOKA, Sekino Shrine. Toyama Prefecture.

At this festival there are seven *yama* floats and the people are proud of the beauty, originality, and traditional use of them. Seven surrounding towns enter into the festival activities and are extremely zealous in maintaining the uniqueness of each *yama*. Even the music from each area is traditional to that particular section.

May 1

UESUGI (SHRINE) MATSURI

At YONEZAWA, Uesugi Shrine. Yamagata Prefecture.

An annual shrine event in which there is a costume parade originating in feudal days and a *mikoshi* drawn by an ox.

May 1–5

HAMAMATSU ODAKOAGE or Big Kite-Flying

At HAMAMATSU, Suwa Shrine. Shizuoka Prefecture.

Held as part of the annual Suwa Shrine Festival. The kite-flying event dates back to about 1550 when a baby son was born to a feudal lord. He announced the fact to all by writing the name of the child on a kite and flying it so that all could see it. During the five days of the festival, young men from each ward of the city assemble with their kites of all sizes and descriptions and engage in a "kite battle." The contestants are expert kite-fliers; their kites fly to right and left with remarkable speed. The biggest attraction is on the last day when more than sixty areas have kites in the air and each flier tries to cut down the kites of the others by means of sharp objects or bits of glass attached to his kite string. The day just happens to coincide with that of Boys' Day, and this event adds interest to the day as celebrated in Hamamatsu. (See page 146.)

May 1–5

DAINEMBUTSU KYOGEN

At KYOTO, Shinsen-en Shrine. Kyoto Prefecture.

Masked pantomime plays.

May 2

SHOMUSAI MATSURI

At NARA, Todaiji Temple. Nara Prefecture.

This is a beautiful festival in memory of the death of Emperor Shomu (701–756), founder of the temple. On the morning of May 2, there is a long procession of priests, children, men, and women, dressed in the costumes of the Nara and Heian periods.

Kites do battle in Hamamatsu; contestants try to cut the strings of their opponents' kites by means of abrasive string. (May 1–5.)

May 2–4

MIZUSAWA KOMAGATA MATSURI
At MIZUSAWA. Iwate Prefecture.

An annual spring shrine festival featuring a *mikoshi* parade on the last day. There are also a cavalcade of horses and a children's armored-costume parade.

May 3

CONSTITUTION DAY. National Holiday

This is a comparatively new holiday for the Japanese people. It is set aside to commemorate the day on which the new national constitution was put into effect. Government offices, large business organizations, and schools are closed. In the morning a great mass meeting is held at the area in front of the Niju-bashi Bridge (Tokyo), at the entrance to the Imperial Palace. The function is participated in by the general public, high officials, and the emperor and empress.

May 3–5

DONTAKU MATSURI or Holiday Festival
At FUKUOKA. Fukuoka Prefecture.

A popular fete participated in by large numbers of city people and attracting crowds from surrounding areas. Fancy-dress processions and many geishas take part. There are floats, dancers in legendary demon-god costumes, variety shows, a children's parade, a cavalcade of horseback riders, and even a talent show. The main procession is on the first day at ten o'clock and goes to the Kushido Shrine. This holiday used to be held during the New Year holiday season—hence the name.

May 3–5

HIMEJI OSHIRO (CASTLE) MATSURI
At HIMEJI, Himeji Castle. Hyogo Prefecture.

Himeji Castle is the very famous "White Heron" Castle, now completed after eight years of restoration work. Features of the festival include a parade of daimyo lords, an automobile parade of notable citizens, and a variety of shows and special events.

May 4–5

AGEUMA SHINJI or Steeplechase Event
At KUWANA. Mie Prefecture.

Kuwana was one of the fifty-three stages on the old Tokaido Road. The event commemorates the time when warriors had to be trained in horseback riding, but today teams from various surrounding sections compete in steeplechasing. If riders can clear the bars successfully, a good crop will result. On the first day there is a parade of horsemen dressed as ancient warriors; and on May 5, a *chigo* parade and the divination event.

May 5

TANGO-NO-SEKKU or Boys' Day
(See Chapter 9 for full description.)

May 5

KODOMO-NO-HI or Children's Day. National Holiday

A relatively new holiday set aside to honor all children of the country and to wish them happiness and prosperity. It is a day set aside to bring attention to the importance of respecting the character of children and of children expressing their gratitude to parents.

May 5

FUCHU KURAYAMI MATSURI or Night Festival

At FUCHU, Okunitama Shrine. Tokyo Prefecture.

This shrine (also called Rokusho) was founded in 113 A.D., but the present buildings date from the middle of the seventeenth century; the gigantic trees along the approach to the shrine date from 1614. A very popular annual night festival.

May 5

KAMO HORSE RACE

At KYOTO, Kamigamo Shrine. Kyoto Prefecture.

An annual horse-riding ceremony.

May 7–8

MISASA HANAYU MATSURI or Flower Spa Festival

At MISASA (Spa). Tottori Prefecture.

Misasa ranks second among the celebrated hot springs in Japan. The springs are efficacious for relieving digestive organ diseases, rheumatism, and neuralgia. The spa has a festival to Yakushi, god of medicine. Some of the events celebrated are a flower market, tug of war, float parade, geisha parade, lantern parade, and fireworks display.

May 8

NABEKAMURI MATSURI or Pan-on-Head Festival

At SAKATA, Chikuma Shrine. Yamagata Prefecture.

This festival is one of the most unique of all the *matsuri* celebrated. Its origin goes back to the time when a girl who had been married before came into the town wearing a pan on her head. One feature in a parade carries out this idea: twelve children (*chigo*) wear huge papier-mâché pans on their heads and tied under their chins. Other participants in the parade are those wearing No play costumes, lion dancers, drummers, flutists, and girls who carry sacred mirrors.

148

May 10

SHIMOTANI (SHRINE) MATSURI

At TOKYO, Shimotani Shrine. Tokyo Prefecture.

Tokyo's largest *mikoshi* placed on a cart is pulled by large groups of children who take turns in going to various areas of the city.

May 11

CORMORANT FISHING SEASON BEGINS

On NAGARA RIVER. Gifu Prefecture. And on UJI RIVER. Kyoto Prefecture.

Ukai, or fishing for *ayu,* a kind of fresh-water trout, is a national feature that is celebrated in Japan from about this time until about November 15. This method of catching fish, used for centuries, is unique in that cormorants are used for catching the fish, which are attracted to them by the light of a fire on the end of a stick that is hung out over the water from a small fishing boat. The spectacle is always crowded, and reservations should be made in July and August to see it.

Cormorants catch fish and yield them to their masters in Gifu Prefecture's famous annual event. Fish are attracted by lighted fires suspended from the boats. (May 11.)

May 11–12

KOFUKUJI TAKIGI NO

At NARA, Kofukuji Temple. Nara Prefecture.

These No plays, given by the light of fires at night in an open-air area, are the oldest form of such entertainment in Japan. Masters from five famous No schools perform by the light of *takigi* (bonfires).

May 12

MYOCHOJI (TEMPLE) CELEBRATION

At KAMAKURA, Myochoji Temple. Kanagawa Prefecture.

A memorial service with special events to honor the Priest Nichiren, founder of the Nichiren sect of Buddhism.

May 12

NERIKYO or Requiem Procession

At KOBE, Taisanji Temple. Hyogo Prefecture.

Many devotees, wearing masks and ancient costumes, have a procession in the precincts of the temple.

May 13–15

NANAO SEIHAKUSAI or Blue Oak Tree Festival

At NANAO, Ochinushi Shrine. Ishikawa Prefecture.

This festival is known for its huge *yama*. It takes many days to assemble them. These *yama* are not only as high as a two-story building but they are constructed without nails or pegs; only strong wisteria vines hold them together. It is said that about four hundred years ago carpenters in the town were ordered to build good *yama* and in return they would be released from taxation. This explains the origin of the first ones. On the front of each one Kabuki dolls are arranged in tableaux; each year the scenes are changed. On the night before the festival, some of the dolls to be used are decorated at homes where there has been a recent wedding or at a new home, and people go to enjoy the sociability and to watch the process of the decorations. On May 14, everyone goes to the *yama* parade (it takes several hundred men to pull all of them), in order to see the results of the many days spent in preparing them.

May 13–16

KOMATSU OTABI MATSURI or Travel Festival

At KOMATSU, Uhashi and Hiyoshi Shrines. Ishikawa Prefecture.

Legend has it that some people went south from Komatsu to Lake Biwa and there saw plays performed on *yama* and were so impressed that they copied them. There are now eight *yama*, and each year plays are performed

on two of them by little girls, aged seven to twelve. The unique part is
that they first have a parade to the shrines in their costumes; then return
to take part in the Kabuki plays, plays that are usually acted by men.
On the fifteenth there is a *mikoshi* parade accompanied by children, about
fifty lion dancers, and an ancient costume procession of over three hundred
people on decorated trucks. Although this is primarily a children's festival,
adults lend ample encouragement to the success of the event.

May 14–16

MINATO MATSURI
At YOKOHAMA. Kanagawa Prefecture.
> A festival held in memory of the opening of Yokohama to foreign trade
> in 1858. A masquerade parade starts from the Chamber of Commerce at
> 1 P.M. and goes through the streets for two and a half miles to Maita Park.
> There many bands play, including the United States Army band.

May 14–15

OGAKI MATSURI
At OGAKI. Gifu Prefecture.
> There are festival floats upon which dolls are manipulated like puppets.
> At night the floats are lighted with hundreds of lanterns and are paraded
> through the streets.

May 14–16

KANDA MYOJIN MATSURI
At TOKYO, Kanda Myojin Shrine. Tokyo Prefecture.
> This shrine festival has been regarded as one of the two greatest *matsuri*
> of its kind in the capital city, the other being the one at the Hie Shrine.
> During the Edo period, both shrines were substantially supported by the
> Tokugawa shoguns. On May 15, there are more than twenty glittering
> portable shrine *mikoshi* representing the parishioners' districts, and the par-
> ticipants stage spirited demonstrations in carrying them in the procession.
> The very long parade also visits several sections of the city during the three-
> day festival. Important local personages join the parade, as do priests on
> horseback and musicians. Performances of *dengaku* (ancient dances) also
> add to the gaiety of the event.

May 15

AOI MATSURI or Hollyhock Festival
At KYOTO, Kamigamo and Shimogamo Shrines. Kyoto Prefecture.
> One of the most important festivals held in Kyoto. (See Chapter 3 for
> full description.)

May 15–16

SANJO DAIMYO GYORETSU or Daimyo (Feudal Lord) Parade
At SANJO. Niigata Prefecture.

> Children's daimyo parade and *mikoshi* parade. As part of the latter, there are two groups, one trying to keep the *mikoshi* on the ground, the other trying to lift it to their shoulders; this provides a noisy, lively spectacle.

May 15–17

RICE-PLANTING FESTIVAL
At KOCHI CITY, Wakamiya Hachiman Shrine. Kochi Prefecture.

> Many local districts have various ways of celebrating the rice-planting festival, but an unusual one is held at this shrine in the sacred rice paddy of the shrine. Several hundred men take part in the ceremonial planting of rice. But on the first day of the ceremony, women are the absolute rulers of the community, and this continues for a three-day period. They take wooden buckets, fill them with mud from the rice paddies, and throw the mud at every man in sight regardless of his business or profession. (See also Chapter 13: RICE AND OTHER FOOD FESTIVALS.)

May 16–18; Variable

KUROFUNE MATSURI or Black Ship Festival
At SHIMODA, Gyokunsenji Temple. Shizuoka Prefecture.

> Commemorating the first landing of Commodore Perry from his American "black ships," this annual festival is held at Kurofune Square. The affair, begun in 1934, has now become one of the major festivities of this part of the country.

May 17

WAKAYAMA WAKA MATSURI
At WAKANOURA. Wakayama Prefecture.

> Wakanoura, a seaside resort near the city of Wakayama, is one of the most scenic places in Japan. The Kii Channel is on one side and the mountains on the other. Here is held a succession of performances: children's group singing, the singing of seamen's songs, demon dances, and sword drills, among others. The procession starts about 1 P.M. (variable) and proceeds to Wakayama Castle in the center of the city. The castle was built in 1585 by Shogun Toyotomi Hideyoshi.

May 17–18

SANJA-SAMA MATSURI
At TOKYO, Asakusa Shrine. Tokyo Prefecture.

> A festival held to honor three fishermen brothers who are said to have been the founders of the Asakusa Kannon Temple more than thirteen centuries

ago. The event is reminiscent of the atmosphere of the latter part of the nineteenth century when Tokyo was still Edo and the neighborhood of Asakusa Park was one of the most popular amusement centers of the capital. During three days, more than fifty magnificent portable shrines of all sizes and descriptions are shouldered to honor the three brothers (*sanja-sama*). On this occasion, the young men exert their strength to the utmost, as the *mikoshi* are extremely heavy. The bearers reel from side to side, drifting toward each other and away, as though quarreling. The Asakusa Shrine has three portable shrines of its own, one for each deified spirit of the

The town of Shimoda celebrates the arrival of Commodore Perry and his "black ships" in a commemorative event each year. (May 16–18, variable.)

three fishermen. During festival days three parties of priests in full-dress Shinto robes make the rounds of all the districts on horseback, each leading one of the portable sacred shrines. At the Asakusa Shrine, there are performances of sacred dances, and prayers for good harvests, a reminder that Tokyo was once a farming area.

May 17–18

GRAND FESTIVAL OF TOSHOGU SHRINE

At NIKKO, Toshogu Shrine. Tochigi Prefecture.

This festival is held with great pomp and ceremony, reproducing a scene of the days of the Tokugawa shogunate regime when at its zenith. The procession includes Shinto priests, court nobles, warriors, musicians, and many others. This main event, the *Sennin-Gyoretsu* (procession of one thousand persons), is also celebrated on a minor scale on October 17. (See Chapter 4 for full description.)

May 18–19

TOTTORI HIJIRI (SHRINE) MATSURI

At TOTTORI, Hijiri Shrine. Tottori Prefecture.

The festival includes an armor parade, more than forty floats, lion dancers, and dance groups from all parts of the city.

May 19

BOMMO-E

At NARA, Toshodaiji Temple. Nara Prefecture.

The ceremony observes the anniversary of the death of Kakusei, twenty-first chief priest of the temple. At the end of the memorial service and the presentation of sacred dances, round, open fans (*uchiwa*) are hurled down from the balcony to be picked up and taken home by visitors who wish to have them as a talisman against misfortune.

May 19–21

MIKUNI MINATO MATSURI or Port Festival

At SAKAI, Mikuni Shrine. Fukui Prefecture.

The original purpose of the festival was to attract people to the shrine. The festival today includes *dashi* or festival floats that are pulled through the streets from each section of the city. There is also a parade of costumed warriors and *mikoshi*.

May 22

SHORYO-E

At OSAKA, Shitennoji Temple, Rokujido Hall. Osaka Prefecture.

A Buddhist service dedicated to Prince Shotoku, founder of the temple.

Classical music is played by temple musicians and sacred dances are performed on stage in front of the hall.

Third Sunday in May

MIFUNE MATSURI or Boat Festival

At KYOTO on Oi River near Arashiyama. Kyoto Prefecture.

Calendar of Japan's Festival Year

The emperor and his courtiers used to make frequent boat trips down the river to view the beautiful scenery of Arashiyama. This festival commemorates that time. Gaily decorated boats, on which the bowsprits are in the form of dragons and phoenixes, float down the river carrying musicians. The parade originates from the Kurumazaki Shrine, goes through the streets, across the Togetsukyo Bridge, and onto the boats. Other features of the event include a *chigo* parade, tea ceremony, flower arrangement exhibits, and showings of other representative arts.

May 24–25

YUSHIMA (SHRINE) MATSURI

At TOKYO, Yushima Shrine. Tokyo Prefecture.

An annual event at which traditional *sato-kagura* (sacred dance pantomimes) are performed to ancient music.

May 25

NANKO MATSURI

At KOBE, Nanko Shrine. Hyogo Prefecture.

Also called Loyalist Nanko's Festival. It is held in praise of Kusunoki Masashige, a loyalist of the feudal age. Special ceremonies and a parade are held.

May 28

FUDO TEMPLES MATSURI

At TOKYO. Tokyo Prefecture.

All Fudo temples hold festivals on this day, the most popular ones being those of Meguro-ku and Koto-ku, Tokyo. The festival is a picturesque one with thousands of people making pilgrimages to the temples in holiday attire to pray for peace in the country and prosperity for their families.

May 30

Sunday (Approximately)

OIGAWA RENDAI-WATASHI

At SHIMADA. Shizuoka Prefecture.

This event is reminiscent of the Edo era, when there was neither bridge nor ferry across the Oi River from Shimada to Kanaya on the other bank.

Travelers had to be carried on the shoulders of watermen or in a sort of sedan chair called a *rendai*. In memory of this time, the annual event is known as *rendai-watashi*, which means "carrying a *rendai* across the river" (Oi River). On this Sunday, a costumed daimyo and his retinue are carried in a palanquin which is put on a float and taken across the river. Spectators can (for a fee) also cross the river on a float. A *mikoshi* is also carried across by many strong-armed young men. (This festival is suspended in some years.)

June 1–2

TAKIGI NO
At KYOTO, Heian Shrine. Kyoto Prefecture.
No plays are presented in the outdoors after dark by the light of blazing *takigi* torches. Attracts many spectators. Actors are from five famous No schools, and the presentation in open air gives an entirely different atmosphere and unusual aspect to the performances.

June 1–25

ITAKO AYAME MATSURI or Iris Festival
At ITAKO. Ibaraki Prefecture.
Iris flower exhibit on Saturdays and Sundays during the period; also iris dances by geishas, singing contests, haiku poetry readings, and photography contests. Many lanterns are hung on the banks of the river nearby, presenting a beautiful evening scene. (See also Chapter 14.)

June 2

ENNEN-NO-MAI or Longevity Dance
At NIKKO, Sambutsudo Hall of Rinnoji Temple. Tochigi Prefecture.
Performed by priests clad in beautiful silk robes, wearing short swords, and carrying fans. Supposed to represent the ancient *dengaku* dances of the Kamakura period (twelfth century).

June 2

RINNOJI (TEMPLE) MATSURI
At NIKKO, Rinnoji Temple. Tochigi Prefecture.
Annual colorful festival.

June 4–5

YAMASHIRO SHOBUYU or Iris Bath Event
At KAMA, Ishikawa Prefecture.
On June 4, scores of young men carry *shobu mikoshi* around the public baths at the Yamashiro Spa. In due course, when the baths are opened for

the public, bales of iris (*shobu*) leaves are thrown into the water, thus supposedly disposing of evil. *Ryokan* (inns) are decorated with special curtains (*mammaku*); and the eaves of inns, homes, and other places are decorated with iris leaves and red lanterns. On a specially constructed stage, geishas dance and young men beat time with drums. Although a month later, this date probably coincides with the Iris Festival (May 5) connected with Boys' Day. (See also Chapter 14.)

June 5–6

AGATA (SHRINE) MATSURI
At UJI, Agata Shrine. Kyoto Prefecture.

Agata Shrine, a branch of the Byodoin Temple, noted for its evangelical zeal, has an unusual festival held at midnight with no lights. About 150 young believers carry a huge paper ball to the shrine and observe a ceremony of transferring a god to the *bonten* (inner shrine). (Visitors must apply to the shrine office to see the ceremony.) On the way back to the start of the parade, paper bits are scattered from the *bonten* and people try to pick them up, thus being assured of happiness and prosperity.

June 5–6

YOBUKO OTSUNAHIKI or Big Tug-of-War Event
At HIGASHI MATSUURA. Saga Prefecture.

Two teams, one representing the land and one the sea, engage in a tug of war; if the land team wins, there will be a good harvest; if the sea team wins, the fishing season will be good.

June 5–12

SHIRANE TAKOGASSEN or Kite-Fighting Event
At SHIRANE. Niigata Prefecture.

About three hundred years ago the banks of the Nakanoguchi River (a branch of the Shirane River) had to be built up, and in celebration of completion of the project, kites were flown. About this time of year, depending on the wind, huge kites are flown (about fifteen by twenty feet in size), and spectators sometimes help in flying them. Smaller kites are flown also, and these engage in air battles. Kite merchants may be seen along the riverbanks. Since the kites bear advertisements, as many as possible are flown, until the air seems to be completely filled with them.

June 6–9

EBARA (SHRINE) MATSURI
At TOKYO, Ebara Shrine. Tokyo Prefecture.

The culmination of the three-day festival is the observance of the *kappa matsuri* (or sea monster festival) which is held on June 8, 10 A.M., when the spirited young fishermen carry out large portable shrines into the sea off the coast of Tenno-su, Shinagawa, to invoke the blessing of the sea god for the prosperity of the fishing season. Shinto music can be heard amïd cheers of spectators on the beach. On the sea off the coast, hundreds of gaily decorated vessels and pleasure boats may be seen. A unique, exciting festival.

June 10

OITA HIRUKO MATSURI
At OITA, Hiruko Shrine. Oita Prefecture.
This *mikoshi* sea procession is surrounded by over three hundred boats decorated with streamers. At night, small bonfires are lighted on the ships.

June 12

TSUYU or Rainy Season
The rainy season begins about this date and continues for about a month. *Tsuyu* as written in characters is literally translated into English as "plum rain," so-called because the fruit of the plum tree ripens during this season. The season is especially welcomed by rice-growing farmers.

June 13–15

HYAKUMANGOKU-SAI or Lord's Million Measures of Rice Event
At KANAZAWA, Oyama Shrine. Ishikawa Prefecture.
Now the capital city of the prefecture, Kanazawa was once a small village (Yamazaki) near the present Kenroku Park. Beginning with 1580, it remained under the Maeda clan for three hundred years. One feature of the festival is a parade showing the first lord coming into the area. Other sections of the event include a talent show, geisha entertainment, an Oyama Shrine *mikoshi* parade, old-world firemen with children dressed as firemen, demonstration of fire techniques, drum parades, art exhibits, an advertising float parade with about two hundred merchants participating, a tea ceremony demonstrated by masters of various tea ceremony schools, and, in the evening, No drama performed by actors of the Hojo school.

June 14

RICE-PLANTING FESTIVAL
At OSAKA, Sumiyoshi Shrine. Osaka Prefecture.
A group of twenty young women dressed in traditional kimonos plant rice seedlings in the sacred paddy fields of the shrine accompanied by music and songs. Thousands of people throng around the fields to witness the ceremony. Similar festivals are held in many rural areas of Japan at this time of year. (See also Chapter 13: RICE AND OTHER FOOD FESTIVALS.)

158

June 15

CHAGU-CHAGU UMAKO
At MORIOKA. Iwate Prefecture.

This festival, with a name derived from the sound of bells hung on horses, is a kind of horse festival, since they are considered so important to agriculture. Beautifully-dressed boys and girls ride in a parade on decorated horses led by white ropes. A picture of a horse is offered to the local shrine and prayers are made for the safety and well-being of horses.

June 15–17

SANNO MATSURI
At TOKYO, Hie Shrine. Tokyo Prefecture.

During this period the shrine compound is a colorful scene with crowds of people making pilgrimages to the shrine in holiday dress. On June 15, the shrine mobilizes its portable shrines and gilded lions' heads as a part of the festive rites. Each section in the surrounding area sends a *dashi* (festival float or cart) for the main parade. The festival is usually held every other year and alternates with the Kanda Myojin Matsuri, Kanda Myojin Shrine, Tokyo, May 14–16.

Although they are not frequently seen in festival parades, women participate in the Sanno Matsuri, which emanates from Tokyo's Hie Shrine. (June 15–17.)

159

PEIRON (BOAT) RACE

At NAGASAKI, Nagasaki Prefecture.

Calendar of Japan's Festival Year

The *Peiron,* a unique and exciting boat race, which is believed to have its origin in China, is regarded as one of the most interesting events held in Nagasaki. The race is so desperately contested that it draws great crowds from neighboring cities. The bowsprit is painted black, the bulwark vermilion and white. When speeding, the craft looks much like a centipede in action. It is manned by thirty-five men, and there are gong-beaters and drummers to assist them in maintaining a regular rhythm. The course is long and strength and skill are required in order to outstrip opponents.

To the rhythm of many drums like these, oarsmen compete in the large boats of Nagasaki's Peiron (Boat) Race Festival. (Mid-June.)

Mid-June

KEMARI or Kick-Ball Event

At KOTOHIRA. Kagawa Prefecture.

The history of this type of game goes back one thousand years; suspended during the Meiji era, the game has now been revived. Six men dressed in ancient court costumes play a round of twenty to thirty minutes during which time the leather ball is kicked (no use of hands) and is supposed to be kept in the air at all times. There are old-time yells as the game progresses. The harmony of movement, the costumes and the sounds of the spectators, all remind the people attending of ancient customs. There is no winning or losing; it is just an interesting game revived from previous centuries.

June 15–16

MIKOSHI MATSURI

At SAPPORO, Sapporo Shrine. Hokkaido Prefecture.

A three-*mikoshi* parade with many participants in historic costumes, something like the Jidai Festival on a minor scale. It is a popular event, with thousands in attendance.

June 20

BAMBOO-CUTTING CEREMONY

At KYOTO, Kurama Temple. Kyoto Prefecture.

A sixteenth-century serpent is the legendary foundation of this event in which two teams, an east and a west team, engage in a thrilling competition to cut long bamboo poles (representing the serpent) into three pieces, this being done with sharp swords. When cut, the winning team rushes to the temple. It is a kind of divination ceremony, for if the east team wins, the Omi district will have a good harvest; if the Tanba district wins, that section will have ample crops.

June 21

ATSUTA (SHRINE) MATSURI

At NAGOYA, Atsuta Shrine. Aichi Prefecture.

Tourneys of sumo, judo, etc., are held in the daytime. After dark, beautifully decorated straw boats with many lanterns are set afloat on the river near the shrine. The fireworks display is extremely spectacular and many thousands come to see it.

June 24

IZONOMIYA OTAUE MATSURI
At SHIMA, Izonomiya Shrine. Mie Prefecture.

A feature of this *otaue* (rice-planting) festival centers around the shrine's sacred rice paddy, where little children get in little boats on the water and beat drums. Groups in appropriate dress enact in pantomime the various processes involved in the growing of rice. (See also Chapter 13: RICE AND OTHER FOOD FESTIVALS.)

June 28

SOGADON-NO-KASAYAKI
At KAGOSHIMA. Kagoshima Prefecture.

This event is named for and relates to the names of a famous father and sons; the father was killed by the samurai and the sons avenged his death. It commemorates filial respect and loyalty for the father. In this event, boys visit homes and collect old umbrellas, after which they make a huge pile of them by the river and then set fire to it. As the flames rise higher and higher, spectators sing a song about the Soga brothers.

June 30

SUMIYOSHI (SHRINE) MATSURI
At OSAKA, Sumiyoshi Shrine. Osaka Prefecture.

A colorful annual festival held each year at the shrine. This shrine has so many stone lanterns, gifts of sailors and shipowners, that it is a rare spectacle to see them lighted during this fete day. The shrine is dedicated to four Shinto deities, three of which are worshiped as guardians of sea journeys.

July 1

SEASON FOR CLIMBING MOUNT FUJI
The season for climbing Mount Fuji begins on July 1 and closes on August 31. More than sixty thousand people, including foreign visitors, scale the mountain during the two summer months. Mount Fuji may be climbed by day or night, but many prefer to start at night in order to reach the eighth station in time to see the sunrise.

July 1–15

HAKATA YAMAGASA
At FUKUOKA, Kushida Shrine. Fukuoka Prefecture.

The city is divided into two parts by the Naka River, with Hakata on one side and Fukuoka on the other. This festival involves not only the townspeople in the two places and other nearby areas but dollmakers of the famous Hakata dolls as well. The *yama* used at this event are called *yamagasa* and in this case are quite different in that beautiful new dolls are made for them each year, mostly by the assistance of the (clay) dollmakers. After the dolls are completed they are put on display for all to see; then the *yama*, with dolls in place, are taken to other towns in the nearby areas. The climax is on July 15 when the *yamagasa* parade goes first to the shrine of Fukuoka, circles about, then returns to the two temples. Later in the day, the shrine presents a traditional No play.

July 3

GRAND ANNUAL FESTIVAL
At MOUNT SHIGISAN, Chogosonshi Temple. Nara Prefecture.
> The largest festival of the year in the area. Splendid view from the summit.

July 3–7

TANABATA (Weaving Loom) or HOSHI (Star) MATSURI
At HIRATSUKA. Miyagi Prefecture.
> This popular festival is held in many places; these events have many similar aspects. See August 6–8 for the same festival in Sendai, considered one of the most outstanding of its kind. (See Chapter 11 for full description.)

July 5

JUFUKUJI MATSURI
At KAMAKURA, Jufukuji Temple. Kanagawa Prefecture.
> An unusually interesting annual festival.

July 6–9

FUKUSA TANABATA MATSURI
At TOKYO. Tokyo Prefecture.
> Fukusa celebrates Tanabata (see above, July 3–7) in a modern way, the features of which are: a Miss Tokyo parade, band groups, song groups, and even ballet groups. Held at Nishitamagun, Fukusa-cho, Tokyo.

July 7

HIRATSUKA TANABATA MATSURI
At HIRATSUKA. Kanagawa Prefecture.
> Another modern version of a Tanabata celebration, with a Miss Tanabata parade, police band group, American army band, and, among other features, a photography contest.

July 9–10

SHIMAN-ROKUSEN-NICHI or 46,000 Service

At TOKYO, Asakusa Shrine and Sensoji Temple. Tokyo Prefecture.

A pilgrimage to the temple (or shrine) at this time is said to bring an amount of efficacy equal to that brought by 46,000 visits at other times. The sacred grounds provide a gay site, reminiscent of scenes in old-time Tokyo.

July 9–11

SHIOGAMA SHIP FESTIVAL

At SHIOGAMA, Shiogama Shrine. Miyagi Prefecture.

This annual shrine event is the great festive occasion of the year at Shiogama. It is celebrated to honor the god of the sea so that voyagers and fishermen

A banner-laden bird-boat is the focus of the Shiogama Ship Festival near Matsushima in northern Japan. (July 9–11.)

will be protected. Colorful ships in the shape of phoenixes, with portable shrines on board, go around Shiogama Bay with several dozen attendant ships.

July 10–12

KUWANA ISHITORI MATSURI or "Collect Stones" Festival
At KUWANA. Mie Prefecture.

Once many rocks had to be carried on carts to build a shrine; this "rock-collecting" procedure is the basis for the present *matsuri*. There is a float parade that represents the means by which the rocks were transported, although today's *dashi* are decorated with lanterns, tapestries, and brightly colored cloths. Each float is headed by a group of costumed children. At midnight, all the *dashi* meet together at the shrine, and then each *dashi* returns to the area from which it came. On the eleventh there is a stone presentation to the shrine, after which one procession follows another until the night of the twelfth. At that time all the people gather around the floats, lanterns are lit on them, and then there is a tremendous and thunderous noise of drums that can be heard for miles away.

Calendar of Japan's Festival Year

July 10–12

KOKURA GION TAIKO
At KITAKYUSHU, Yasaka Shrine. Fukuoka Prefecture.

When the rainy season is gone, drums (*taiko*) are beaten to welcome the festival of Yasaka Shrine. For over three hundred years, this fete has been a celebration for peace and safety as well as good harvests. While on a less ambitious scale, it has adapted ideas from Kyoto's Gion Matsuri (see July 16–24). Each town in the area displays its own *yama, hoko,* and drum floats and then goes to surrounding places to show them. From noon to sunset in Chuoko-en (Chuo Park), there is a drum contest.

July 11–12

NOMAOI MATSURI or Horse Festival
At HARANOMACHI. Fukushima Prefecture.

On a moor called Hibarino there is a festival that reproduces a heroic scene of military horsemen in ancient armor and helmet. It is supposed to have originated in a muster of troops of the eight provinces of the Kanto, organized by a former lord of the fief. Eight neighboring villages participate in the event. The principal attraction consists of a procession of shrine floats, a parade of horsemen, and, on the moor, breaking of wild horses, horse races, and games.

July 13–15

BON or O-BON or Feast of Lanterns
Celebrated throughout the country. (See Chapter 7 for full description.)

July 13–15

TOBATA GION MATSURI

At TOBATA. Fukuoka Prefecture.

Four large *yamagasa* festival floats and more than forty smaller ones parade through the city on this day.

July 13–15

HITA GION-E

At HITA. Oita Prefecture.

Yama in the festival parade are decorated with ornate embroidered tapestries and have figures of early-day heroes. Musicians and a drum corps accompany the floats.

July 13–16

YASUKUNI (SHRINE) MATSURI

At TOKYO, Yasukuni Shrine. Tokyo Prefecture.

This festival blends Shintoism and Buddhism and is called Mitama Matsuri or Festival of Departed Souls; it is held within the same period as Bon. In practice both invite the spirits of the dead and pray for their well-being. As a part of the entertainment, a program is given which includes classic No drama, ancient court dances and *Bon-odori* (Bon dances), and geisha dances. Scores of geishas of Fujimi-cho district perform dances, sing, and play samisens. Brilliant fireworks are displayed in the background of the shrine. Young people stage charming dances in rings until late in the night. (See also April 21–25 and October 18–21 for other festivals at this shrine.)

July 14

NATSU MATSURI

At ENOSHIMA (Island). Kanagawa Prefecture.

Portable *mikoshi* are carried by young people, who wade into the sea up to their shoulders and sport about in the waves with them.

July 14

NACHI HI MATSURI or Fire Festival

At NACHI NO TAKI (FALLS), Kumano Nachi Shrine. Wakayama Prefecture.

The most popular festival in the district. Twelve *mikoshi*, each with thirty-eight fans and eight mirrors, leave the shrine and parade to the waterfall. Here the *mikoshi* are welcomed by twelve torch-bearers of the Tobitaka Shrine. The torch fires are used to purify the *mikoshi*, after which ceremonies are held at the foot of the waterfall. At 4 P.M. the *mikoshi* return to the Kumano Shrine. In addition, there are *dengaku* (ancient dance) performances on the evening of the thirteenth and the morning of the fourteenth.

166

July 14

SUMIYOSHI OTAUE SHINJI or Rice-Planting Ceremony
At OSAKA, Sumiyoshi Shrine. Osaka Prefecture.

Young women plant rice seedlings in the shrine paddy field while singing rice-planting songs. Costumes are particularly attractive with flower-decorated hats and red *yukata* kimonos. (See also Chapter 13: RICE AND OTHER FOOD FESTIVALS.)

July 14–15

SUGA (SHRINE) GION MATSURI
At KOSHIRO, Suga Shrine. Saga Prefecture.

Enormous three-storied *yama* are used; the two upper stories are lavishly decorated.

July 15

TAKE-NO-NOBORI
At OGATA. Nagano Prefecture.

In the year 1504 there was no summer rain and the villagers prayed for rain, with the result that the rains came for three successive days thereafter. In gratitude, pieces of cloth of richness and fine color, enough for two kimonos, were offered to the water god. Early in the morning on July 15, representatives of one of three villages (each village has a turn every three years) go up the mountain, and when the sun rises, offer sake and pieces of cloth to the water god. Later they return down the mountain in a gay procession carrying tall poles surmounted by many streamers of cloth of many colors. They are met by the townspeople, lion dancers, and other groups, and a parade ensues.

July 15

ISHIZAKI HOTOSAI or Light-Offering Event
At NANAO. Ishikawa Prefecture.

An offering of tall, many-sided lanterns is made to the Hachiman Shrine and prayers are made hoping to ensure good fishing. Each of six sections of the city have a *kiriko* or huge lantern upon which are pictures and Chinese characters. These are so large that many people are required in order to carry them in a parade. The climax of the event comes when the six *kiriko* meet together at a given area; this happens at night, usually by the light of a full moon.

KANGEN-SAI MATSURI or Music Festival

At ɪᴛsᴜᴋᴜsʜɪᴍᴀ (Island) or Miyajima, Itsukushima Shrine. Hiroshima Prefecture. A colorfully decorated fleet of boats makes a sea parade to the accompaniment of classic court music (*gagaku*). Three boats are joined together with decorated curtains over all, and lanterns are strung between them, just like a "stage on water." Numbers of other decorated boats from other areas around the island cruise the bay to see and listen, thus making a gay sight. At nine o'clock, as people watch from the shrine's outside corridors, the boats return to shore; and at midnight the deity that had been carried on one boat, is returned to the shrine. Before ending the festival, the fleet of boats makes three last circles around the shrine.

Calendar of Japan's Festival Year

Seen against the lovely wooded island of Miyajima and the hills of mainland Honshu, the many boats of the Kangen-sai Festival comprise an unusual aquatic spectacle. (July 16–17.)

July 16-24

GION MATSURI

At KYOTO. Kyoto Prefecture.

> This is one of the main festivals of the year, one of the largest held in Japan, and a "must" for all who can arrange to see it. (See Chapter 6 for full description.)

July 20

SUITOSAI or Festival of the Canals

At OSAKA. Osaka Prefecture.

> The festival is held in Sakuranomiya and Nakanoshima parks, celebrated with unusually spectacular night fireworks displays.

Miyajima's Itsukushima Shrine, its famous red *torii* immersed in the water, is the locale for the weird and ancient *gagaku* dances. (July 16-17.)

TOGO SUIGO MATSURI or Watery-Area Festival
At TOGO. Tottori Prefecture.

Once in 1579 a battle was lost here and the lake became red with the blood of the many casualties. The warriors who survived started a memorial service that has continued through these many years. In the evening on this date, thirty memorial ships are launched on the lake. Lanterns are set afloat on the water, an offering to the souls of those who perished in the battle. Torch fires are burned on the shores of the lake and dances are presented with the villagers as active participants.

July 20–22

KUMAGAYA UCHIWA MATSURI or Open Fan Festival
At KUMAGAYA. Saitama Prefecture.

Kumagaya was a stopping-place on the old road to Tokyo in the early days, and guests were entertained and also given rice cooked with red beans. Later, the *ryokan* (inns) gave open fans instead of rice to the guests; this custom has continued. During the two festival days, there is a *mikoshi* and *dashi* parade and fans are the main decoration; even the city seems to be flooded with fans during this *matsuri*.

July 20–24

TAKAMATSU MINATO MATSURI or Port Festival
At TAKAMATSU. Kagawa Prefecture.

In addition to a costume parade and several kinds of exhibitions and events (some in Ritsurin Park), there is a boat race in the harbor.

July 20–27

YAMAGUCHI GION MATSURI
At YAMAGUCHI, Yasaka Shrine. Yamaguchi Prefecture.

A lord of the Ouchi family built numerous splendid temples in imitation of Kyoto, which it resembles topographically. Kyoto's Gion Matsuri served as a pattern for the one held here. The *mikoshi* are of various shapes: octagonal, hexagonal and square—an unusual feature, as is the "Heron Dance" presented prior to the procession.

July 22–23

FUKUSHIMA MIKOSHI MATSURI
At NISHICHIKUMA, Minase Shrine. Nagano Prefecture.

Legend relates that once when two men brought *mikoshi* to the shrine, they were pursued by two law officers. In their anxiety to escape, they threw the *mikoshi* into a valley and escaped to Fukushima. Today, new *mikoshi* are made; there is a parade on July 22, but the next day they are thrown away, as in the legend. There is great boisterous behavior on the part of the participants as the *mikoshi* are rolled back and forth until broken. Half-broken ones are then taken to the shrine. A performance of dancing and singing is given.

July 23

MATSUNO-O (SHRINE) MATSURI
At KYOTO, Matsuno-o Shrine. Kyoto Prefecture.

   Rice seedlings, first presented at the shrine, are then transplanted by young women in traditional costumes. The seedlings are believed to be charms against insects that might harm rice crops.

July 23–24

WAREI NATSU MATSURI or Summer Festival
At UWAJIMA, Warei Shrine. Ehime Prefecture.

   A guardian god of fishermen and farmers is enshrined in the Warei Shrine. Prayers at the shrine are offered asking for good fishing and ample harvests. For two days, decorated boats from many places in the general area come to join in the summer festival in this port city. There are land and water *mikoshi* parades, a bullfight, and other events; and at night, torch-light-bearers and fireworks.

July 24–25

MATSUMOTO TENJIN MATSURI
At MATSUMOTO. Nagano Prefecture.

   In this old castle town (1583) there is a time-honored procession with about twenty *dashi* in the main parade.

July 25

TANEGASHIMA (ISLAND) TAIKOYAMA MATSURI
At NISHI-NO-OMOTE, Yasaka Shrine. Kagoshima Prefecture.

   The *mikoshi* of Yasaka Shrine, flag-decorated, is taken to a neighboring shrine accompanied by four child drummers. In order to reach this shrine, a river must be crossed; unless the drummers beat hard and fast, the *mikoshi*-bearers dip the *mikoshi* into the water.

July 25–26

YAHIKO TOROSHINJI or Lantern Offering
At NISHIKANBARA, Yahiko Shrine. Niigata Prefecture.

   On the evening of July 25, more than twenty *toro* (hanging lanterns) are brought to the shrine. The lanterns are huge; upon them smaller lanterns are hung; and all are decorated with artificial flowers. As the young men start moving the *toro*, crowds of people dance around the decorated lanterns. At ten in the evening when the shrine priests appear, villagers join in the lantern parade. When all return to the shrine again late at night, a performance of dancing and singing is held on a special shrine stage.

July 25–26

TENJIN MATSURI

At OSAKA. Osaka Prefecture.

One of the largest of Japan's summer festivals. It is unique in that it has both a land and sea procession. (See Chapter 2 for full description.)

July 25–27

AIKAWA KOZAN MATSURI or Mine Festival

At SADO (Island). Niigata Prefecture.

Famous for its early-day mining activities. The present festival has been initiated for the purpose of attracting visitors and features: *dashi* parade, songs, dances, and a parade in costume. All events are held in the town of Aikawa.

July 31

FIGHTING FESTIVAL

At OITA. Oita Prefecture.

This festival, also known as Kenka Matsuri, is so-called because it is marked with terrific fights among the carriers of three portable shrines. The fights are due to a religious idea that if one of the three shrines gets to the Sacred Place of Sojourn first, the district represented will receive a greater divine blessing for its inhabitants than will the others. Late in the afternoon the hundred young men assemble in the compound of the Usa Shrine and get ready for the journey to the Sacred Place, a distance of five blocks. Fierce wranglings ensue as the carriers try to get ahead of each other. When the shrines finally arrive at their destination, they remain there for two days before returning to the Usa Shrine. During the interim, music, dances, and various forms of entertainment are performed.

July 31

HAKONE JINJA (SHRINE) MATSURI

At HAKONE, Hakone Jinja (Shrine). Kanagawa Prefecture.

The festival is held on Lake Ashi, and the function attracts visitors from this and other nearby areas. Late in the afternoon, the chief priest, attended by assistants and parishioners, observes elaborate rites on boats, rites that symbolize the feeding of a dragon in order to appease it. Following the ceremonies, parishioners and visitors float thousands of lighted paper lanterns on the water and set them adrift toward the outlet of the lake. In addition there are various forms of entertainment and also fireworks displays.

July 31 and August 1

SUMIYOSHI (SHRINE) MATSURI

At OSAKA, Sumiyoshi Shrine. Osaka Prefecture.

A special feature of the festival is a *Miscanthus* (ornamental grass) ring through which people pass who wish to be protected from any evil. *Mikoshi* are put on carts and pulled by automobiles (a modern touch). They form a parade at 9 P.M. and return to the shrine at midnight. During the day, a historical parade with costumed participants and musicians and floats constitutes an important part of this Osaka summer festival.

August 1

ICHINOSEKI MATSURI

At ICHINOSEKI. Iwate Prefecture.

Summer festival celebrated in connection with Tanabata and the opening of the Iwai River with fireworks displays.

August 1–2

GERO ONSEN MATSURI

At GERO SPA. Gifu Prefecture.

At one time the spa was one of the most famous of the hot springs areas for medicinal efficacy and baths. A few years ago, a new festival was initiated to attract visitors. On the banks of the nearby Masuda River, a concert and fireworks display are given as well as Bon dances and a ceremony of gratitude for the hot springs. On August 2, there is a children's *mikoshi* parade and a geisha parade.

August 1–3

KUSATSU ONSEN MATSURI

At AZUMA. Gumma Prefecture.

A ceremony of thanks for the hot springs (*onsen*); water is taken from the main hot springs and distributed in scoops to five nearby districts by *miko* (Shinto maidens). Other features of this comparatively new festival include a "Miss Kusatsu" carriage pulled by oxen, ceremonial court music (*gagaku*), and evening bonfires.

NEBUTA MATSURI

At AOMORI and HIROSAKI. Aomori Prefecture.

The feature of this extraordinary festival held by two cities is the procession of monstrous dummies (*nebuta*) of men, animals, birds. This is said to have originated in a legend that when Sakanoue-no-Tamuramaro, a famous war-

The violent play of lines in this float-borne image of legendary personages gives life to the Nebuta Matsuri of Aomori. (August 1–7.)

rior, was dispatched to the northeastern part of the country to lead the imperial forces some ten centuries ago in order to quell a rebellious tribe, he had numerous *nebuta* set up and hilarious demonstrations made to entice the enemies out of hiding. When they came out, the imperial forces captured them. In Aomori, children make paper lanterns and carry them through the streets at night. On the third or fourth day there are parades in both cities with scores of carts conveying *nebuta* representing men and animals. The two cities are scenes of gaiety during the entire holiday week.

August 1–7

PILGRIMS' FESTIVAL
At NIKKO, Mount Nantai. Tochigi Prefecture.

The festival consists of a visit to the three shrines on Mount Nantai. Pilgrims first cleanse themselves in the lake. The climb is made from Chugushi (the middle shrine at Lake Chuzenji) at midnight. Pilgrims dressed in white and carrying lanterns make an unusual sight. The object is to get to the top, a five-mile steep ascent, by sunrise. About ten thousand pilgrims make the trip during the first week of August.

August 1–7

BIWAKO MATSURI
At OTSU (and other towns in the area). Shiga Prefecture.

Cities around Lake Biwa participate in the festival, in which twelve representatives secure fire from a shrine. In each city and town around Lake Biwa, there are sumo tournaments, talent shows, fireworks, and a lantern reception to the members of the "thanks mission" or fire-carriers of the various twelve areas.

August 4

MIYA MATSURI or Shrine Festival
At KYOTO, Kitano Tenjin Shrine. Kyoto Prefecture.

Annual summer shrine festival.

August 5

LAKE KAWAGUCHIKO MATSURI
At MINAMITSURU, Kawaguchi Lake. Yamanashi Prefecture.

Villagers hold an annual lantern fete with fireworks displays. Lighted ships circle around and zigzag across the lake. At the close of the festival, flowers are thrown into the lake to comfort those who accidentally drowned in it. A fine view of Mount Fuji, as it stands majestically inverted in the lake, may be seen from the north shore.

August 5

HAKONE TORII MATSURI
At LAKE HAKONE. Kanagawa Prefecture.

Once people threw *torii*-shaped paper into the river for the purpose of ensuring safety in travel; now a huge *torii* lighted with about a thousand lanterns is set afloat on the lake in this festival in order to accomplish the same purpose.

August 5–7

YAMAGUCHI TANABATA CHOCHIN MATSURI
At YAMAGUCHI. Yamaguchi Prefecture.

During this lantern (*chochin*) festival this prefectural capital city is combined with a Tanabata celebration. Hundreds of bamboo poles with elaborate paper decorations may be seen and thousands of lanterns are used as archways over the streets.

August 5–7

TAKAOKA TANABATA MATSURI
At TAKAOKA. Toyama Prefecture.

The night scene of this Tanabata celebration is especially impressive, as is the scene afterward, when the one thousand or more paper-decorated poles float down the Chiho River nearby.

August 6

PEACE FESTIVAL
At HIROSHIMA. Hiroshima Prefecture.

The most important event held in this city; begun in 1947. The purpose is to console the souls of the dead and to pray for permanent world peace. The opening ceremony is held by the memorial tomb that bears the inscription, "Please sleep peacefully; we shall never make the same mistake again." Notables lay wreaths and a peace declaration is read. At 8:15 A.M. (time of the bombing), with the signal of the peace bell, sirens sound and bells join in, as people sing songs of peace. People along the banks of the river pray; sutras are read and little lighted paper lanterns float down the river.

August 6–7

KANTO MATSURI or Balancing Festival
At AKITA. Akita Prefecture.

The feature of this spectacular evening festival is the manipulation and balancing of the so-called *kanto*, a huge bamboo framework in the shape

176

of a mast, about thirty feet tall with nine crossbeams at regular intervals upon which lanterns are hung. A huge *kanto* has a capacity of forty to fifty lanterns and may weigh as much as eighty pounds. On August 5, the young men in all districts make the *kanto* for their respective districts. When finished, the young men stage stunts in balancing the *kanto* on their chins, heads, foreheads, for the entertainment of the crowds. The park where this is done is a picturesque sight with thousands of young people in holiday attire who not only come to see the spectacle but who engage in general merrymaking, singing popular songs to the music of flutes, samisens, and drums.

August 6–7

WARAKU ODORI (DANCE)

At NIKKO. Tochigi Prefecture.

One of the most famous and popular folk dances in Japan. On the nights when the performances are given near the Waraku Pond, tens of thousands of people gather to observe and to dance to the accompaniment of gay music.

August 6–8

TANABATA (Weaving Loom) or HOSHI (Star) MATSURI
At SENDAI. Miyagi Prefecture.

This popular festival, held in July in many cities, is considered the most outstanding such celebration in the country. (See Chapter 11 for full description.)

August 6–8

SUMIYOSHI (SHRINE) MATSURI
At TOKYO, Sumiyoshi Shrine. Tokyo Prefecture.

An octagonal portable shrine is taken around the one-time island area by a large vessel escorted by a number of small boats. On August 7, in the afternoon, a number of large gilded lion heads are brought into the shrine compound to start on a journey through neighboring villages. Members of fishing villages have a strong attachment to the Sumiyoshi Shrine because the object of worship to which the shrine is dedicated has been their guardian deity for hundreds of years. It is claimed that all people in this area are related, for it is their belief that their guardian deity does not wish any of their people to leave the area to live elsewhere. The islands lying off Tsukiji (Chuo Ward, Tokyo) may be reached by bridge or ferry. Sumiyoshi Shrine is located on Tsukuda-jima, once a small fishing village off the coast of Tsukiji.

August 7–13

SUHODEI MATSURI

At SHIMONOSEKI, Inomiya Shrine. Yamaguchi Prefecture.

A little before sunset many young men and women gather at the shrine, the men carrying sixty-foot poles with long streamers, and the women with colorful lanterns. Afterward they dance together and there is gay native music.

August 8–9

KAMAKURA CARNIVAL

At KAMAKURA, Yuigahama Beach. Kanagawa Prefecture.

The annual event is promoted by a prominent group of residents and supported by the Kamakura municipality and various other institutions interested in railway and tourist industries. The event has all the elements of a carnival including a "Miss Carnival" parade with the runners-up as attendants to the carnival queen. There is a fishing contest for children, a male-female baseball game, a pageant, dog show, fashion show, ballet, and photography contest, flower arrangement exhibits, and a fancy-dress parade.

August 9–12

KOCHI YOSAKAI MATSURI

At KOCHI. Kochi Prefecture.

The title of the festival is derived from the name of a famous folk song of this area. Thirty-six hundred or more people dance in the streets, making the event competitive with the Awa Odori (Dance) at Tokushima.

August 13

YARI MATSURI or Spear Festival

At OJI. Nara Prefecture.

Dedicated to Prince Izanagi and Princess Izanami, the mythical divine couple who gave birth to the islands of Japan. On this day at the shrine, miniature spears are given as offerings and a festival is held in connection with the event.

August 13

YAIZU-NO-ARAMATSURI or "Rough" Festival

At YAIZU. Shizuoka Prefecture.

A type of "quarrel" festival in which twenty-four *mikoshi* and several hundred *mikoshi*-bearers are involved. Their behavior is rough (*ara*), as indicated in the title of the *matsuri*.

August 13–16

GUJOHACHIMAN BON-ODORI
At GUJO, Gujo Town Hall. Gifu Prefecture.

The origin of the dance festival dates back to the time (1624–1643) when a feudal lord used to have community dancing for the purpose of maintaining harmony between farmers, merchants, and the samurai. Today, during this three-day period, all-night dances are participated in by thousands who come in their summer kimonos. There is a several-storied stage upon which the musicians sit. The event is becoming nationally known and is more popular each year.

Calendar of Japan's Festival Year

August 14–15

HIEDANO (SHRINE) SAEKI TORO or Lantern Festival
At KYOTO, Hiedano Shrine. Kyoto Prefecture.

A festival with a three-hundred-year tradition. The combined *mikoshi*, drum float, and lantern parade is a night festival, thus avoiding the heat of a summer day.

August 14–19

HIGASHIYAMA BON-ODORI
At AIZUWAKAMATSU. Fukushima Prefecture.

Bon dancing on a large scale with villagers from adjacent areas participating. Prizes are given for the best costumes and the best dancers.

August 15

MANDO-E or Lantern-Lighting Ceremony
At NARA, Kasuga Shrine. Nara Prefecture.

Thousands of lanterns are lighted at the Kasuga Shrine on this night—and on February 3.

August 15

TORO-NAGASHI or Lantern Offering
At TOKYO, Asakusa Temple. Tokyo Prefecture.

The temple holds its annual service by the Sumida River by the nearby Kototoi Bridge. It is held in conjunction with the Bon season to comfort the spirits of those who died in wars and by water. Several hundred lighted lanterns (square and mounted on boards) are floated down the river while Buddhist priests chant sutras.

179

August 15

FUKAGAWA HACHIMAN MATSURI

At TOKYO, Tomioka Hachiman Shrine. Tokyo Prefecture.

Over fifty large and small *mikoshi* parade around sections of the Tomioka district. At Fukagawa there are geisha dances, traditional since the Edo period. Once in three years, a much larger parade is part of the festival.

August 15–17

YAMAGA TORO MATSURI or Lantern Festival

At YAMAGA, Omiya Shrine. Kumamoto Prefecture.

Once an emperor had to find his way through fog by means of torchlight; this is the basis for the lantern festival. Paper lanterns used in this festival are quite different in that no bamboo is used, only paste. Each section of the city vies with the others in producing the best and the most beautiful lanterns. When finished, an exhibition of them is held in each area. Other features of the festival include Bon dances, fireworks, sports contests, lantern dances, and a variety show (held at the Yamaga Primary School). At the Omiya Shrine, *kagura* (sacred) dances are performed all night. At midnight all the lantern-bearers meet at the shrine, and at four o'clock in the morning they return to their respective sections of the city.

August 16

DAIMONJI OKURIBI or Great Bonfire Event

At KYOTO, Mount Nyoigadake. Kyoto Prefecture.

On a hill behind the Zenrinji Temple and facing Kyoto, a great bonfire is constructed in the shape of a Chinese character meaning "big." The origin of the custom is attributed to an apparition of the burning of a temple at the foot of the mountain. The horizontal stroke of the character measures 230 feet and the left vertical stroke 510 feet, the right one, 408 feet—a magnificent sight when set on fire. This is only one of such events in this and other areas. Two similar ones on the same date may be seen at Yokote City, Akita Prefecture, and at Mount Myojo, Hakone, Kanagawa Prefecture. Since it is Bon season, the idea behind such events is that the fires will light the souls of the dead as they return to the other world.

August 16

MATSUSHIMA TORONAGASHI or Lantern Event

At MATSUSHIMA. Miyagi Prefecture.

Matsushima, the pine-clad island, so-named from the hundreds of pine-clad islets in the bay, is one of the scenic spots in Japan. Here there is a time-honored custom on this day of setting sail many thousands of little boat-lanterns on the smooth waters of the bay.

The character for "big" written in fire astride a Kyoto hillside illuminates the city on the night of August 16.

August 16

ONI-MAI or Demon Dance
At SOSA. Chiba Prefecture.
 The villagers present seven plays dealing with hell and the hereafter, with somewhat realistic details.

August 16

MIYAZU TORONAGASHI or Lantern Offering
At MIYAZU. Kyoto Prefecture.
 Here it is believed that souls come from the sea and return to the sea, and for this reason a day is set aside to aid spirits returning to the other world. In the evening, as sirens sound, lighted lanterns are set afloat in the bay. Fireworks are set off from a ship in the bay and on shore sutras are said; then Bon dances are performed. For an hour or more, the bay is aflame with the burning lanterns. Matsuzaki Park is the best place from which to see the event.

August 18

OJIKA KUJIRA MATSURI or Whale Festival

At OJIKA. Miyagi Prefecture.

> This is a fisherman's festival to encourage a season of good fishing. A huge whale made from papier-mâché is the main feature of the parade and there are opportunities to hear and see dancing and singing.

August 18

TAMATORI or ENNEN-SAI or Ball-Catching Festival

At ITSUKUSHIMA (Island), Miyajima, Itsukushima Shrine. Hiroshima Prefecture.

> Hundreds of men and boys dive after a sacred wooden ball flung into the sea. The one who captures the ball and delivers it back to the shrine receives gifts and is thus supposed to attain happiness and health.

August 21–23

NIIGATA MATSURI

At NIIGATA. Niigata Prefecture.

> The festival has a two-hundred-year history, but several years ago it was decided to make it more than a local port festival. Today the events include: opening of the Shinano River (originated after 1923), with appropriate ceremonies; a commerce and industry parade (new); anniversary of opening of the harbor (new); fireworks display; a folk-song parade which marks the opening of the festival itself with five thousand people in seventy-five groups' participating; a *mikoshi* parade; one hundred geishas from fifty various sections and one hundred advertisement floats.

August 22–25

AWA ODORI DANCE FESTIVAL

At TOKUSHIMA. Tokushima Prefecture.

> This famous dance festival (formerly held at Awa, hence the name) possesses such vigor and charm that it will remain in the memory of all who see it. Regarded as one of the national events in Japan, it attracts thousands of visitors. Many troupes of dancers participate; it is difficult to find any Japanese festival more truly festive. There is dancing and parading in the streets day and night during the three-day period.

August 23

HANASE MATSURI GYOJI or Pine Throw Event

At KYOTO, Kasuga Shrine, Sakyo-ku. Kyoto Prefecture.

> Here is a festival entirely different from any other in the country. A huge umbrella is put on a sixty-foot-high pine tree and the idea is for young

men to throw torches up to the umbrella to set fire to it. As a result, the pine tree is consumed by fire as well.

August 24

DAIMYO MATSURI or the Lord's Festival
At YUZAWA. Akita Prefecture.
    A procession of feudal lords and their retinues as they appeared in feudal days; also *dashi* and *mikoshi* floats.

August 24

KUMOGAHATA AGEMATSU GYOJI
At KYOTO, Kita-ku, Mount Atago. Kyoto Prefecture.
    A festival similar to the Hanase Matsuri (above, August 23) except that there is a thirty-foot pillar on which there are torch fires in the shape of Chinese characters. The characters are changed each year.

Awa Odori can be seen in city districts, where tireless dancers perform far into the night. One of the most famous places to see *Awa Odori* is in Tokushima, Tokushima Prefecture. (August 22–25.)

JOKOMYOJI HIWATARI or Fire-Walking Rite
At KAMAKURA, Jokomyoji Shrine. Kanagawa Prefecture.
    Five bundles of firewood are set ablaze and the shrine priests walk across
the bed of coals, the idea being to demonstrate that fire can be controlled.
(See September 17, *Chinkashiki*, Tokyo, Koma-Zawa Shrine.)

At the Suwa Shrine at Ishiki, Aichi Prefecture, hours are consumed in lighting
what probably are Japan's largest paper lanterns. (August 26–27.)

ISHIKI OCHOCHIN MATSURI or Lantern Festival
At HAZU, Suwa Shrine. Aichi Prefecture.

A local legend tells of a dragon who used to appear along the shore, annoying people. To put a stop to it, a big bonfire was made and the sea creature destroyed. After that, bonfires were built in commemoration of the destruction of the legendary dragon. So many bonfires were built that it was decided to use lanterns instead. The day before the festival, six groups of believers from different sections of the city install three enormous pillars in the Suwa Shrine compound. By means of strong pulleys, a pair of huge lanterns are raised and hung on the poles. These lanterns, which date from the Edo period, are thirty feet high and about eighteen feet across; smaller ones are twenty feet high and twelve feet in diameter. At night the priests light the large lanterns, which takes many hours. On the last night the lanterns are taken down after a performance of *kagura* (sacred) songs and dances.

Calendar of Japan's Festival Year

August 26

FUJI-YOSHIDA HI MATSURI or Fire Festival
At FUJI-YOSHIDA, northern foot of Mount Fuji, Sengen Shrine. Yamanashi Prefecture.

Toward evening on the festival day, dozens of bonfires are lighted in areas of the city. On Mount Fuji, bonfires are lighted at many places along the climbing path. Young men carry a vermilion-lacquered portable shrine through the streets. It is modeled in the shape of the famous Mount Fuji. Five days later the Mount Fuji climbing season closes.

Late August and Early September

INSECT-HEARING FESTIVALS

A picturesque rite that has come down from feudal days. This is a pastime held in temple and shrine precincts, public parks, and many gardens at the time when the "seven grasses of summer" are in full bloom. People gather in chosen spots where they take insects in tiny bamboo cages, some of which are purchased from insect vendors for the ceremony of "freeing the insects." As the insects are set free, the liberator waits for them to get their bearings, realize their freedom, and then listen to them as they burst forth with their chirpings. There is a festival on May 28 at which time the insect vendor sells his wares. People seem to enjoy keeping the insects close at hand during the summer months in order to enjoy their sounds during the evenings. This custom is probably much more prevalent in rural areas.

185

September 1–3

YATSUO KAZE-NO-BON or Wind Bon Event
At NEI-GUN. Toyama Prefecture.

In ancient days the people thought during the typhoon season that an evil god sent the violent storms, and so they devised certain ceremonies and dances to appease the typhoon-causing god. This is no longer believed, but the people still have a festival, just for pleasure. On the first and second nights, the men and women of eleven villages in the area assemble at Yatsuo Primary School where dances are presented on a specially constructed stage. The third night is less formal; all dance who wish to do so and the streets are full of dancers.

September 1–3

JINJA MATSURI or Shrine Festival
At HACHINOHE. Aomori Prefecture.

A joint festival of three shrines, Ogami, Shiragi, and Shinmei-kyu. There is a *mikoshi* and *chigo* parade.

September 3–5

UMI MATSURI or Ocean Festival
At KITAKAMI-GUN. Aomori Prefecture.

The festival includes a *dashi* and *mikoshi* parade on September 3 and 5, and the main attraction, an ocean *mikoshi* event on the fourth.

September 8–10

SHISHIMAI or Lion Dance Event
At ISHIOKA CITY, Soja Shrine. Ibaraki Prefecture.

Besides a *yama* float procession, a famous Lion Dance (*shishi*) is a feature of the festival.

September 9

IKUDAMA (SHRINE) MATSURI
At OSAKA, Ikudama Shrine. Osaka Prefecture.

Annual fall festival. The shrine is noted for its fine view of the city.

September 9

CHOYO-NO-SEKKU or Chrysanthemum Day

This was once an important festival day, on which the feudal lords were expected to call on the shogun. The emperor used to hold banquets on this day but it is not celebrated to any extent any more, except for com-

186

petitive chrysanthemum shows held about this time in many cities. (See Chapter 14: SEASONAL FLOWERS AND OTHER DISPLAYS.)

September 11–13

NINGYO MATSURI

At MITO. Aomori Prefecture.

Each section in Mito makes a doll and puts it on a twenty-foot *dashi* float. People parade along with the *ningyo* floats.

September 11–13

FESTIVAL OF ST. NICHIREN'S PARDON

At ENOSHIMA, Ryukoji Temple. KAMAKURA, Botamochi Temple. Kanagawa Prefecture.

This day is set aside to honor the memory of St. Nichiren, considered to be the most zealous priest in Japanese Buddhism. He carried on a vigorous missionary campaign with Kamakura as the center of activity for the spread of his faith, while denouncing all other sects. He so offended government authorities that he was sentenced to be beheaded, but lightning struck near the execution site, causing officials to reconsider. At length he was exiled to Sado Island, until his final release on September 12, 1271. From that time on he began to propagate what is known as Nichiren Buddhism. The sect has several million members today. The celebrations today are marked by thundering demonstrations: thousands of devout men and women, each with a fan-shaped drum, shout Nichiren prayers in accompaniment to the beating of drums. At Kamakura, parishioners make an offering of *botamochi* or rice balls coated with sweet bean paste. The grand festival of the temple called *Oeshiki* (Hommonji) in Tokyo is held on October 12 in commemoration of the death of St. Nichiren. Thousands of believers march to the temple carrying *mando* (literally "ten thousand lights") that are mounted on poles and decorated with artificial flowers.

September 11–21

GINGER FESTIVAL

At TOKYO, Daijin-gu Shrine. Tokyo Prefecture.

This is a historic event dear to the hearts of old-time Tokyo citizens. It is so-called because many merchants sell, among other things, fresh ginger. A special article sold is *chigibako* or a set of three small boxes of graduated size, decorated with flower designs, a simple toy-box for girls. At this shrine, as at other noted shrines in Tokyo, there is a major festival on the even years and a minor festival on the odd years. During the major festivals, the shrine compound is jammed with holiday-makers with large groups of geisha girls who sing and dance, and there is a portable shrine parade.

187

Prowess in archery on horseback and in classical costume is demonstrated in the *yabusame* event of the Hachiman Shrine, Kamakura. (September 14–17.)

September 13

MYOHONJI (TEMPLE) MATSURI

At KAMAKURA, Myohonji Temple. Kanagawa Prefecture.
Annual autumn festival celebration.

September 14–17

HACHIMAN (SHRINE) MATSURI

At KAMAKURA, Hachiman Shrine. Kanagawa Prefecture.

At TAKAYAMA, Hachiman Shrine. Gifu Prefecture.

High-wheeled floats, elaborately decorated with gold and carvings, are used in processions. The festival is featured by *yabusame,* an interesting arrow-shooting game played on horseback, a reminder of feudal days when samurai warriors vied with each other in horsemanship and archery.

September 15

IWASHIMUZU (SHRINE) MATSURI

At OSAKA, Iwashimuzu Shrine. Osaka Prefecture.

One of the oldest shrines in Japan. On this festival day, participants wear ancient court costumes prevalent in the Heian period (794–1185), and set birds (and fish) free at the shrine. The same ceremony takes place at Kyoto, Iwashimuzu Shrine.

September 15

UNEME PROCESSION

At NARA. Nara Prefecture.

This is an unusual procession, held to comfort a former court lady, Uneme, who held an unrequited love for an emperor. Priests in purple robes, girls in white veils, and children with flowers parade through the streets, go around the lake, and stop at a willow tree, the supposed trysting place of the lovers. There the participants sing hymns, and in the evening a flower-decorated fan is presented to the shrine and prayers are offered for Uneme.

Mid-September

TSUKIMI or Moon-Viewing

The practice of greeting the moon is not observed so generally as it was in times past. However, even in the heart of Tokyo, some families still observe the custom as an annual feature. Late in the afternoon, just before twilight, the housewife places a low table on the veranda or perhaps on the window sill, where the full moon will shed its rays, and upon it spreads an offering to the moon. Rice balls, *o-dango,* are put on the tray together with a vase containing the "seven grasses of autumn," cooked vegetables, chestnuts, and fruits. When the moon rises, members of the family and guests sit near the table, admire the beauty of the moon, and enjoy some refreshments. The festival is an old custom and has no religious significance. A three-day moon-viewing festival is held in the *Hyakka-en* or Garden of One Hundred Flowers, at Mukojima, Sumida-ku, Tokyo. The midautumn moon is regarded by the Japanese people as the clearest and most beautiful of the year.

September 15–16

MUGIYA MATSURI or Wheat-Dealer Festival
At TONAMI-GUN. Toyama Prefecture.

The Johana section of this district began a festival ten or more years ago and introduced the *mugiya* dance (the origin of the name of the festival dance is unknown, but it is believed to have been inherited from the *Heike* warriors). The dance is a combination sword-umbrella dance, and men in formal costume with sword and umbrella perform. There is a practice session during the afternoons; the performance is given later that day at the Zentokuji Temple and the primary school. Some people dance in the lantern-decorated streets and visitors are invited to dance also.

September 15–16

TSURUGAOKA HACHIMAN (SHRINE) MATSURI
At TOKYO, Tsurugaoka Hachiman Shrine. Tokyo Prefecture.
Main annual festival celebration.

September 17

CHINKASHIKI or Ceremony of Fire Control
At TOKYO, Koma-Zawa and other shrines and temples in Japan. Tokyo Prefecture.
The purpose of the ceremony performed by Shinto priests who walk on fire beds is to demonstrate that fire can be controlled and rendered helpless to believers. Prayers to conquer fire are offered as priests slowly and solemnly march around the charcoal bed of coals, until they work themselves into a state akin to ecstasy. Each priest then takes salt, casts it into the fire, rubs salt on his feet, steps upon the surface of the burning charcoal, and strides over it with dignified gait.

September 20; Variable

HIGAN or AUTUMN EQUINOX DAY. National Holiday
During the week centering around this day, Buddhist temples hold services in honor of the dead. People visit cemeteries for the biannual cleaning-up of the graves and to pray for souls of the departed and honored ancestors. The emperor pays respects to his ancestors on this day also. *Higan* means "other shore"; it is believed that the land of Amida Buddha or Buddhist

190

paradise is situated in the west, the direction in which the sun sets. On the day of autumn equinox the sun sets due west, and for this reason, people emphasize their belief in the "other land."

September 22–24

AIZU MATSURI

At AIZUWAKAMATSU. Fukushima Prefecture.

Calendar of Japan's Festival Year

Once Aizu was considered the strongest fortress in northeast Japan, but the castle here was destroyed during the Restoration period. Here is the burial place of the *Byakkotai* or White-Tiger Band, a group of youths who swore with their lives to protect the castle against imperial troops. Seeing a fire rising from the castle, they thought it had fallen into the hands of the enemy and so kept their vow by taking their own lives. Today this city memorializes this event by having a procession of the *Byakkotai* and a lantern procession.

September 23

HIROSAKI RINGO MATSURI or Apple Festival

At HIROSAKI. Aomori Prefecture.

A recreational festival of people engaged in apple-growing. Events include folk dancing, a lion dance, and a *dashi* parade.

September 23–25

YAMANAKA ONSEN MATSURI

At YAMANAKA SPA, ENUMA-GUN. Ishikawa Prefecture.

The Yamanaka Spa, so proud of the scenery along the beautiful Daishoji River, celebrates its festival with folk-dance teams that dance in the streets of the city all hours of the night; there are also a lion dance and a *dashi* parade with costumed participants and geishas.

September 23–25

ISE SHRINE KAGURA MATSURI or Sacred Dance and Music Festival

At ISE, Ise Shrine. Mie Prefecture.

A sacred dance called *kagura* is performed in the halls set apart for this purpose, the Butterfly Dance (*kocho-no-mai*) being one of the famous ones.

September 25–27

YOKKAICHI MATSURI

At YOKKAICHI, Suwa Shrine. Mie Prefecture.

A daimyo (feudal lord), *mikoshi* parade, and two unique floats, one depicting the catching of whales and one with men wearing animal skins, are the chief features of the festival occasion.

September 27

ANKOKURONJI (TEMPLE) MATSURI
At KAMAKURA, Ankokuronji Temple. Kanagawa Prefecture.
Annual festival of the temple.

September 30 and October 1

NARUGO KOKESHI MATSURI or Wooden Doll Festival
At NARUGO-CHO, TAMATSUKURI-GUN. Miyagi Prefecture.

This area has a tradition of *kokeshi* doll production. On the evening of the thirtieth there is a memorial service for *kokeshi* dolls. There are discussion groups, a dance contest, a meeting to honor those contributing to the industry, a talent show, and fireworks. On the second afternoon there is a *mikoshi* attended by geishas, and a fancy-dress parade.

October 1–3

HOJOTSU YAMA MATSURI or Float Parade
At SHIMMANATO, Hojotsu Hachiman Shrine. Toyama Prefecture.

The festival celebration dates back to 1697, when thirteen *yama* floats from surrounding areas came to celebrate at this shrine. Today the *yama* have lavish lacquer and gold decorations. Lanterns on them in the evening add to their luster and beauty. On the second day, in the shrine compound, a stage is set up with pine trees as a backdrop for a doll exhibit: a goddess doll wearing a demon mask, with four dolls dressed as guards or *shiten-no*.

October 1–4

KITANO (SHRINE) MATSURI
At KYOTO, Kitano Tenjin Shrine. Kyoto Prefecture.

The annual festival of the shrine is held in honor of Sugawara Michizane, statesman and scholar of the latter part of the eighth century, revered by the Japanese people as the deity of learning and deified under the name Tenjin. The festival is noted for its interesting procession of townspeople in holiday attire and shrine cars decorated with such vegetables as the *zuiki* and stalks of the *satoimo* (a kind of taro).

October 1 to December 1

NAGAME KIKU-NINGYO or Chrysanthemum Doll Show
At YAMADA-GUN. Gumma Prefecture.
OSAKA, Hirakata Recreation Park. Osaka Prefecture.

Variety show and chrysanthemum doll show; dolls made entirely of chrysanthemum flowers. There are other such shows at this season. (See Chapter 14: SEASONAL FLOWERS AND OTHER DISPLAYS.)

October 2–17

OSAKA CITY FESTIVAL

At OSAKA. Osaka Prefecture.

Each day special events are scheduled; parades representing the procession of Toyotomi Hideyoshi (1536–1598) when he entered Osaka Castle which he had built; a feudal lords' procession of the Edo period (1615–1868); a masquerade parade by Osaka citizens dressed in old and modern dress; a procession of streetcars; and evening fireworks in Osaka Stadium.

October 4–6

NIHOMMATSU CHOCHIN or Lantern Festival

At NIHOMMATSU, Nihommatsu Shrine. Fukushima Prefecture.

On October 4, seven drum carriages precede twenty young men who carry sacred fire from Nihommatsu Shrine and light over a thousand lanterns. At midnight the drum carriages return to the shrine and present welcoming music to the *mikoshi* (with enshrined deity). The next day there is a parade around the city and the participants separate into groups and go to nearby towns.

October 5–28

AUTUMN KAMOGAWA ODORI

At KYOTO, Ponto-cho Kaburenjo Theater. Kyoto Prefecture.

Geisha dancing and representative dances of various areas of Japan. Three performances daily and four on Sundays.

October 8–9

MIKAWA-MIYA MATSURI

At GAMAGORI. Aichi Prefecture.

In 1696, a man had a dream in which an enshrined deity was taken from Hakken Shrine to a shrine in Wakamiya. Interpreted as a personal message, he made a simple sacred float, transferred the spirit-deity to it and thence to the Wakamiya Shrine. Today, the several communities in the general area build their *mikoshi* and are held responsible for some type of entertainment for the festival. In addition to a parade and dancing, four of the *mikoshi* are taken by young men into the sea, back to the shrines in the area (even though it may be dark, no lights are used), and then back to the places from which they originated.

October 8

NAGATA (SHRINE) MATSURI

At KOBE, Nagata Shrine. Hyogo Prefecture.

Annual autumn festival of the shrine.

Nagasaki's Okunchi Festival, with its imaginative dragons, shows the Chinese roots of the Japanese culture. (October 8–9.)

October 8–9

OKUNCHI MATSURI

At NAGASAKI, Suwa Shrine. Nagasaki Prefecture.

A notable festival, originated in the seventeenth century when many Chinese lived in the city. Regarded as one of the most distinctive religious festivals in Japan. For three days the streets are filled with processions. Houses are decorated; booths are erected in various parts of the city where jugglers and entertainers perform for crowds that throng from surrounding areas. During the festival many dances of Chinese origin are featured, among which is the Dragon Dance. One belief is that the Tokugawa Shogunate started the festival to draw attention away from the influence of Catholicism, which was being propagated at that time, and so provided people with lavish annual festivals for their enjoyment.

October 9

HASHIGO-JISHI or Ladder-Lion Event
At AICHI-GUN, Owaki Shrine. Aichi Prefecture.

A platform with fifty-one steps is constructed; two men disguised as a lion perform extraordinary acrobatics on a steep ladder.

October 9–10

OTSU MATSURI
At OTSU. Shiga Prefecture.

The capital city of Shiga Prefecture, near the entrance to Lake Biwa and therefore an important tourist center, adds to its attractions by holding this two-day festival. It includes: thirteen *dashi* handsomely decorated with black, red, silver, and gold; a parade; and traditional music accompaniment.

October 10

KOMPIRA (SHRINE) MATSURI
At TOKYO, Kompira Shrine. Tokyo Prefecture.

Ten large brass bells hung under the eaves of the shrine are rung by shaking many-colored ropes, and are kept tinkling all day long as pilgrims shake them to attract the attention of the deities so that prayers will be heard. Hundreds of candles are lighted before the shrine altar.

October 9

HANAGASA MATSURI or Umbrella Festival
At KYOTO, Agu Shrine. Kyoto Prefecture.

The main feature of the festival, as the name indicates, is a procession of people carrying extremely large umbrellas decorated with flowers.

October 9–11

KOTOHIRA-KOMPIRA MATSURI
At KOTOHIRA, Kotohira Shrine. Kagawa Prefecture.

The shrine is one of the most popular in the country, second only to the Grand Shrine of Ise in the number of visitors. One of the largest celebrations of the shrine includes: lantern parades, Dance of the Dragon, classic dances by priests and Shinto maidens of the shrine, a *mikoshi* parade that proceeds from the bottom of the hill up a long flight of stone steps to the Kotohira Shrine, and then from the hilltop shrine (about midnight) down to the branch shrine at the bottom. Costumed participants follow along with the parade.

195

October 10

INARI (SHRINE) MATSURI

At KYOTO, Inari Shrine. Kyoto Prefecture.

An autumn festival at one of the most famous shrines in Kyoto.

October 10–11

OSAKA PORT FESTIVAL

At OSAKA. Osaka Prefecture.

A water festival in Osaka Harbor and a costumed feudal lord parade.

October 10–November 20

TAKEFU KIKU-NINGYO MATSURI or Chrysanthemum Doll Festival

At TAKEKU. Fukui Prefecture.

This unusually interesting exhibit of dolls made from chrysanthemum flowers has ten scenes. There are other exhibits, shows, and song performances. The best time to see the doll exhibit is about November 3. (See also Chapter 14.)

October 10–November 30

NINGYODERA NINGYOTEN or Doll Exhibition

At KYOTO, Kamikyo-ku, Hokyoji Temple. Kyoto Prefecture.

The Hokyoji Temple, sometimes called the "Doll Temple" (*Ningyodera*), has an outstanding doll exhibition during this period, a rare sight to see. See also February 15 to March 31, Hokyoji Temple. (See also Chapter 14.)

October 11–12

KAIJOTOGYO-SHIKI or Sea God's Festival

At KOBE, Tarumi-ku, Wadatsumi Shrine. Hyogo Prefecture.

This shrine is dedicated to three Shinto deities who have been worshiped as guardians of voyagers and fishermen. As a consequence, the shrine has a seaside festival in which a sacred shrine is carried on the shoulders of devotees, put on a boat, and launched into Osaka Bay for a water parade, with about twenty other boats following.

October 11–14

OESHIKI or COMMEMORATION OF ST. NICHIREN

At TOKYO, Hommonji Temple. Tokyo Prefecture.

Hommonji Temple is one of the important headquarters of the Nichiren sect of Buddhism. Nichiren's ashes are inurned there, and a commemoration event in his honor is held annually at the temple. No Buddhist event in Japan is quite so frenzied as the service in which the temple priests observe the event, with devotees participating all day and night, led by extremely fervent priests who beat fan-shaped drums and shout prayers. Lanterns some several feet square are mounted on poles, painted with designs appropriate to the sect, decorated with sprays of artificial flowers, and carried in processions around the temple grounds. There are about eight hundred Nichiren societies that participate in this particular event. By nine o'clock in the evening, the spacious compound is a scene of pandemonium, with hundreds of lighted lanterns waving over many thousands of Nichiren followers, who are beating drums and chanting prayers. This continues until the early hours of the morning. See also September 11–13, Festival of St. Nichiren's Pardon.

October 12

USHI MATSURI or Bull Festival

At KYOTO, Osaka Shrine, in precincts of the Koryuji Temple. Kyoto Prefecture. On this night, great crowds go to the temple. A man in a white robe who represents the Madara (God) rides on a bull into the temple grounds. With his followers, he rides three times around the temple before holding a religious ceremony, part of which is the chanting of prayers in archaic languages. There are lantern-carriers, torch-bearers, and some who are disguised as local magistrates, demons, and gods. It is a rather unbelievable event which has a long tradition.

October 13–14

KOMYOJI (TEMPLE) MATSURI

At KAMAKURA. Kanagawa Prefecture.
    Autumn annual festival.

October 14–15

KENKA MATSURI or Quarrel Festival

At HIMEJI, Matsubara Hachiman Shrine. Hyogo Prefecture.
    Enormous shrine *mikoshi* that are carried by teams of parishioners jostle each other for the foremost position in the procession. Since there are elements of danger involved, this kind of festival has been criticized and efforts have been made to decrease the hazards involved. Floats are pulled to the shrine by groups according to ages (those in their forties, thirties, and twenties). At about eleven o'clock in the morning in the compound of the shrine, there is a ceremonial "crushing" of the *mikoshi*, and then they parade for approximately a mile. Then they go to a given area where there is more pushing, with one group attempting to put its *mikoshi* on top of the opponent's *mikoshi*. This "quarreling" lasts about an hour, after which interval a drum corps escorts the *mikoshi* back to the shrine.

Jockeying for the lead position in the procession creates this furor, repeated annually at Himeji's Kenka Matsuri or Quarrel Festival. (October 14–15.)

October 14–November 26

KIKU-NINGYO or Chrysanthemum Doll Festival

At TAKAMATSU. Kagawa Prefecture.

Another of the very unusual chrysanthemum doll exhibits; this one is considered to be the best in Shikoku. (See also Chapter 14.)

Mid-October

SHIKA-NO-TSUNOKIRI or Deerhorn-Cutting Ceremony

At NARA, Kasuga Shrine. Nara Prefecture.

Hundreds of deer of the Kasuga Shrine in Nara are regarded as messengers of the deities of the shrine. They roam about streets, in the woods and dales of the shrine. The horn-cutting is done once a year to prevent them from injuring themselves or possibly visitors who come to see them. The horns are then presented to the shrine and later used commercially in the production of carved objects sold in shops. At the sound of a horn each evening, the deer leave the grassy areas and return to a deer house provided for them in the compounds of the shrine.

October 15

NAGAHAMA MATSURI

At NAGAHAMA, Hachiman Shrine. Shiga Prefecture.

Nagahama, on the east shore of Lake Biwa, has a shrine that presents a noteworthy annual event. The traditional procession of wheeled floats and portable shrines attracts a large crowd.

October 17

TOSHOGU (SHRINE) MATSURI

At NIKKO, Toshogu Shrine. Tochigi Prefecture.

The chief festival of the shrine is held annually on May 17 and May 18; it is considered the minor festival and is conducted on a smaller scale than the spring festival. (See Chapter 4 for description of the major festival, Toshogu Shrine.)

October 17

MINAMI MATSURI

At OSAKA, Sumiyoshi Shrine. Osaka Prefecture.

A "Now and Ages Past" costume parade.

October 17

KANNAME-SAI or God-Tasting Event

It was a traditional day when sake made from new grain and boiled rice of the new crop was offered to the imperial ancestors. It is no longer a holiday and has not been observed for many years, although the ceremony is held at the Imperial Palace and the Grand Ise Shrine.

October 17–18

TSU TAISAI TOJINODORI GYORETSU or Grand Festival and Dance Procession

At TSU. Mie Prefecture.

The festival, which began in the seventeenth century, was once an important one, but was discontinued for a number of years. Recently it has been revived. It is reminiscent of a Korean officers' parade; similar uniforms are worn. Dances believed to be of Korean origin are performed also.

October 19

FUNAOKA MATSURI
At KYOTO, Kita-ku, Kenkun Shrine. Kyoto Prefecture.
> In Funaoka Park there is a parade in which boys wear warrior costumes re-
> plete with armor and which depicts the warrior Oda Nobunaga (end of the
> Ashikaga Shogunate) as he entered into Kyoto.

October 19–21

YASUKUNI (SHRINE) MATSURI
At TOKYO, Yasukuni Shrine. Tokyo Prefecture.
> A shrine on Kudan Hill where people worship the spirits of those who died
> for their country in wars at home and abroad. (See also July 13–16 for de-
> scription.)

October 19

BETTARA-ICHI
At TOKYO, Odemma-cho, Takarada Shrine. Tokyo Prefecture.
> This annual fair is one of the most popular events in Tokyo, perpetuated
> since the Edo period, and is held to supply people with articles necessary
> for the observance of the Ebisu Festival on the following day. On the night
> of the nineteenth, both sides of the street leading to the small shrine are
> lined with stalls selling many kinds of things including "sticky" pickled radish
> (*bettara*).

October 19–20

KAMO TAISAI or Big Festival
At OZU. Okayama Prefecture.
> Shrines from eight surrounding areas join in a major *mikoshi* parade and
> other events. A festival with a long historical tradition.

October 20

EBISU MATSURI or Ebisu Festival
At NARA, Ebisu Shrine. Nara Prefecture.
> So-called after Ebisu, one of the Seven Gods of Luck, patron of fishermen
> and industry. According to legend, Ebisu remains at large during October,
> which is called the "godless month," and all the other gods leave their shrines
> and assemble at the temple of Izumo (Japan Sea, west Japan), where they
> supposedly discuss momentous affairs including arranged marriages. Ebisu
> does not accompany them because, being deaf, he cannot hear the summons.
> October 20 is a day for social gatherings of guild members and political and
> literary societies.

October 20–November 30

KASAMA KIKU MATSURI or Chrysanthemum Festival

At KASAMA, Inari Shrine. Ibaraki Prefecture.

> Over a million people a year come to visit this Inari shrine, one of the three largest of the Inari shrines. In the back of the shrine is a Kiku (Chrysanthemum) Festival, where one of the most elaborate doll displays in Japan is held, with over fifty scenes having dolls made of chrysanthemum flowers. There is an exhibit of the finest varieties of chrysanthemums as well. (See also Chapter 14.)

October 21–22

MINATO MATSURI or Port Festival

At KOBE. Hyogo Prefecture.

> Annual Kobe birthday celebration. Various kinds of events such as: international float parade of decorated automobiles, procession of ages past, parade of illuminated streetcars, and lantern procession on the sea. Commemorates the opening of Kobe to foreign commerce in 1867.

October 22

JIDAI MATSURI or Festival of the Eras

At KYOTO, Heian Shrine. Kyoto Prefecture.

> In commemoration of the founding of Kyoto in 794, Kyoto stages a unique and very elaborate procession of people marching and on horseback who represent the eras of Kyoto's long history. This is one of the most important and largest festive occasions in Kyoto. (See Chapter 5 for full description.)

October 22

HI MATSURI or Fire Festival

At MOUNT KURAMA, north of Kyoto, Kuramadera Shrine. Kyoto Prefecture.

> Long rows of bonfires light the narrow street leading to the shrine. People carry flaming torches of all sizes. This is an extremely unique and fascinating festival. Because of certain current conditions at Mount Kurama, this festival has unfortunately been temporarily suspended. (See Chapter 1.)

October 23–25

IGA UENO TENJIN MATSURI

At UENO, Sugawara Shrine. Mie Prefecture.

> People disguised as demons have a procession to dispel illness and bad luck. This is held on the last day. On the preceding days the events include: a parade of lantern-decorated floats at night, a *dashi* daytime parade, strolling priests (*yamabushi*), a costume parade, and *mikoshi* carried on the strong shoulders of young men.

October 28

TENRIKYO MATSURI
At TENRI CITY. Nara Prefecture.

The headquarters of the Tenrikyo sect of Shintoism is at Tenri City (Tambaichi is the station, 4.6 miles from Nara). The annual festival takes place here on October 26 when more than a half-million adherents of this sect and visitors flock to the city.

October 28–30

OKUNCHI MATSURI
At KARATSU, Karatsu Shrine. Saga Prefecture.

The Karatsu festival, unlike any other in Japan, annually features a float or *yamagasa* parade that was first held in 1819 after a citizen visited the Bion Matsuri, Kyoto, and was so impressed that he and his neighbors built a huge red lion of papier-mâché. By 1876, all fifteen of the small towns in the area entered a float in the *yamagasa* parade. Today, fourteen floats are used; they are tremendous, grotesque, but fascinating papier-mâché figures coated with gold, silver, red, and blue lacquer. On October 28, all of the *yamagasa* meet together and parade around Karatsu City before going to the shrine. On the twenty-ninth (the best day to see the complete parade) and the thirtieth, a huge red lion (built in 1819) heads the procession, followed by a fierce-looking blue lion float (built in 1821). The third float (built in 1844) depicts Taro Urashima, referred to as the Japanese Rip Van Winkle, a legendary fisherman who saved the life of a turtle, was taken to the Paradise of the Sea where he fell in love with the Queen's daughter, and remained there until he finally had a desire to return to his village. When he did, he was unrecognized, for he had been gone for three hundred years. Probably the most impressive float is a gigantic, brilliant red sea bream (or *tai*), a symbol of congratulations as well as a fish well-known for its flavor. A ship float (built in 1846) has an imaginary phoenix (*hoo*) stop; this bird made an appearance only when a country was ruled by a wise monarch, according to the Chinese. An extremely fantastic float (built in 1846) is that of a flying dragon, guardian of the heavens. A gold float with a lion head was added in 1847, as was one of a lion playing ball (in 1875). Four bizarre-looking helmets imitating ones worn by famous warriors are depicted, each one quite different: Minamoto Yoshitsune (built in 1844), Shingen Takeda and Kenshi Uesugi (built in 1869), Raiko's helmet (1869). One float has the Earth Dragon that guards the treasures of the earth, and lastly one of a grampus (or porpoise), both built in 1876. Karatsu is located on a beautifully curved bay with pine-clad beach, and is within the Genkai Quasi-National Park, noted for azaleas in the spring and glorious autumnal colors. It is a superb sight-seeing stop. This entirely unique festival serves to underline reasons for visiting Karatsu City in Kyushu.

The huge red sea bream, symbol of congratulations, is one of the spectacular floats in the Karatsu Okunchi Festival. (October 28–30.)

November 1–15

KITANO ODORI
At KYOTO, Kamikyo-ku, Kitano Kaikan Theater. Kyoto Prefecture.
    Representative dancing groups and music.

Visitors to Hakone, the mountain resort near Mount Fuji, are treated to a parade of ancient lords in the Daimyo Festival. (November 3.)

November 3

HAKONE DAIMYO GYORETSU

At HAKONE. Kanagawa Prefecture.

Local people in costumes of lords, court ladies, warriors, and other groups representative of ancient days, parade through the resort district. Yumoto, one of the oldest towns in the area and a popular hot springs resort, has over a hundred participants in the procession.

November 3

GAGAKU FESTIVAL

At NARA, Kasuga Shrine. Nara Prefecture.

Musicians of the shrine assist with the traditional *gagaku* (court dances) at the Man-yo Botanical Gardens.

November 3

MEIJI-SETSU

At TOKYO, Meiji Shrine. Tokyo Prefecture.

Emperor Meiji, who restored the imperial administration in 1868, is so revered as a great emperor that his birthday (November 3, 1852) is commemorated at this shrine that bears his name. The shrine is dedicated to him and his wife, Empress Shoken (1850–1914). At this time of year the shrine precincts are unusually attractive with the abundance of autumn-tinted maples.

204

November 3

CULTURE DAY. National Holiday

The day is also called *Bunka-no-hi*, a day for the people of Japan to reflect on liberty and peace and to emphasize the importance of promoting culture. In Tokyo, one of the outstanding features of the week that centers around this day is a campaign encouraging the people to cultivate the habit of reading good books. There is a prize contest for the selection of the best ten children's books, technical books, and books of general interest.

November 3–10

SHICHI-GO-SAN CEREMONY

The word *shichi-go-san* means literally "seven-five-three"; the ceremony is observed in families (where tradition is important) who have daughters of seven, sons of five, and sons and daughters of three years of age. It is a charming custom and a delight to see children in these age groups dressed in their finest clothes on the way to various shrines in order to invoke the blessings of the enshrined deities. It is a pleasure for parents to do this because of the pride and thankfulness that their children have attained these ages in sound health and the hope that they may look forward to continued blessings. The most popular shrines for such pilgrimages in the Tokyo area are: Hie Shrine on top of Sanno Hill, the Kanda Myojin Shrine, the Hachiman Shrine in Fukagawa Park, the Hikawa Shrine (Akasaka) and the Meiji Shrine (Yoyogi, Shibuyaku).

November 21–28

HIGASHI HONGANJI (TEMPLE) HOONKO

At KYOTO, Shimogyo-ku, Higashi Honganji Temple. Kyoto Prefecture.

This annual commemoration service in remembrance of the death of Priest Shinran, founder of the Buddhist Shinran sect, is an occasion that draws adherents from all parts of Japan. Every day throughout this period there are services with sutras and prayers for the dead.

November 22–23

SHINNO MATSURI

At OSAKA, Higashi-ku, Sukunahikona Shrine. Osaka Prefecture.

Shinno was a Chinese medicine god and Sukunahikona a Japanese medicine god. In 1822, when cholera was prevalent, the dealers in drugs made a medicine and presented it in a papier-mâché tiger (since the medicine was made from the bones of a tiger's head) to the shrine. In turn, those who were ill with cholera received the medicine. Today, there is no need of such medicine but about a thousand small papier-mâché tigers are made and distributed to the people. In addition, there are about a hundred tall poles decorated with paper strips, much like those used in Tanabata celebrations, that are paraded through the streets.

November 23

LABOR-THANKSGIVING DAY. National Holiday

November 23 is the *Kinro-kansha-no-hi,* or Labor-Thanksgiving Day, a new national holiday that combines the Western observance of the two holidays. It is a day for people to express gratitude for success and abundance, to reflect on the dignity of labor, and to congratulate one another upon successes of the past year.

Three Times During November

TORI-NO-ICHI or Fowl Market

No temple or shrine festival in November is more colorful nor more like those of the early Edo period (1603–1868) than Tori-no-ichi, so-called because it takes place on the Day of the Fowl in November. The event calls direct attention to the fact that the year is drawing to a close and that preparation should be made for the New Year's holidays. This affair is one that has survived with little change. It takes place at all Otori shrines in Tokyo and its suburbs as well as elsewhere, but the best-known one is situated at Ryusenji-machi, Taito-ku, Tokyo. The principal article sold at the market— and you are supposed to bargain rather than pay the asked price—is the *kumade.* This is a colorfully ornamented bamboo rake that contains a variety of good-luck symbols: gold coins, gilded rice sacks, figures of the seven gods of good fortune, cranes, pine trees, tortoises, and many other such charms. These rakes, which are available in several sizes, from those three or four feet in length to some small enough for hair ornaments, are supposed to be kept in the home, place of business, and any other place as a luck-bringer to rake in good fortune.

November 30–December 11

DAITOSAI or Good-Luck Market

At OMIYA, Hikawa Shrine. Saitama Prefecture.

A large market at which many products of all kinds are displayed and at which good-luck charms are sold.

December 1–15

IYOMANTE MATSURI or Bear Festival
At KUTCHARO. Hokkaido Prefecture.

Calendar of Japan's Festival Year

A bear cub is trapped, cared for, fed choice foods. Supposedly the mountain god, *Kimunkamui*, was captured by the devil and placed on earth in the form of a bear; only the death of the bear could set his spirit free again. When the bear is two or three years old, a festival is held. The bear is elaborately dressed on the first day of the festival and there are dancing and ceremonial rites around the wooden-log cage. After that he is led through the village and finally killed. His body is placed in state upon an altar and offerings made to it. This goes on for several days and nights until the last day of the festival, at which time the bear meat is distributed to villagers, the spirit of the mountain god having been released. (The date for this festival is variable and it is not always observed.)

December 1–26

MINAMIZA KICHIREI KAOMISE or Annual All-Star Performance
At KYOTO, Higashiyama-ku, Minamiza Theater. Kyoto Prefecture.

A custom of the Edo era is still in effect whereby Kabuki actors renew their contracts in December; therefore December is considered the first month of the theatrical season. During this season, the best Kabuki plays are presented by the best singers, musicians, and actors; it is the best time of the year to attend such performances. This theater is an excellent place to see the presentations.

December 2–3

CHICHIBU YOMATSURI or Night Festival
At CHICHIBU, Chichibu Shrine. Saitama Prefecture.

The noted *kagura* dance is performed here on December 3, and other festival days. At the time of the festival on this day, elaborate floats are drawn about the street and lavish fireworks are displayed. Since the town is a center of the silk industry (*Chichibu-meisen*), merchants come at this time to see the newest silk fabrics. Features of the festival include: geisha dancers and singers, costumed children, a *mikoshi* and *dashi* parade accompanied by a famous drum and flute group having a distinctive rhythm, and the extensive use of many lanterns.

December 2–13

GION ODORI
At KYOTO, Higashiyama-ku, Gion Kaikan Theater. Kyoto Prefecture.

Talented geishas and *maiko* (young entertainers) of the noted Fujima dance school present performances here during this period. Their costumes are especially colorful and elegant in color and design.

December 3

KOGA CHOCHINMOMI MATSURI, or Lantern-Pushing Festival
At KOGA. Ibaraki Prefecture.
> Young men with sixty-foot poles upon which are lanterns go about the streets pushing each other. In addition to the hundreds of such poles, there are a number of similar but smaller ones for children; on each lantern (*chochin*) there are advertisements.

December 5

SUITENGU (SHRINE) MATSURI
At TOKYO, Ningyo-cho, Suitengu Shrine. Tokyo Prefecture.
> The crowd on this festival day is especially large at this very popular Tokyo shrine. Every fifth day of the month and on the annual festival day on April 15, thousands of people attend festivities at the shrine.

December 13

SUSUHARAI or "Soot Sweeping"
> Since early days there have been those who wish to give their houses a thorough cleaning before year's end. Furniture and utensils that are broken or worn out, and lost articles, all have to be replaced. New chinaware or other articles of housekeeping are substituted for the old, as are worn *tatami* mats or paper sliding doors. In some districts, this is the appropriate time for newly pounded rice cakes (*mochi-bana* or rice-cake flowers) to be tied to willow branches as offerings to the gods. A series of *bonen-kai* or "year-end forgetting parties" are held among friends and employees.

December 13–18

KASUGA WAKAMIYA (SHRINE) MATSURI
At NARA, Kasuga Wakamiya Shrine. Nara Prefecture.
> A short distance away from the main Kasuga Shrine is the Kasuga Waka-miya Shrine, in front of which stands a low, elongated building divided into three sections. The *Kaguraden* is the sacred dancing hall; here the Shinto shrine maidens, each with branches of the *sakaki* (sacred) tree, fans, and a number of tiny bells, gracefully perform the sacred *kagura* dances. The accompanying orchestra is composed of: flute, *koto, sho, hichiriki*, drum, and clappers. The main event is held on the seventeenth in honor of the shrine. It is one of the greatest celebrations in Nara Prefecture. It is characterized by a long procession of warriors clad in armor and many men dressed in costumes of ancient times. The festival draws a tremendous number of spectators from all areas.

December 15–16

SETAGAYA BOROICHI or Trash Market
At TOKYO, Setagaya-ku. Tokyo Prefecture.

Once this event featured a used-clothing and furniture market. Now there are many booths in which general merchandise is sold, including nursery trees and plants, cloth, articles for New Year's decorations and the like, and—reminiscent of the old trash market—some used or discarded items.

December 15–26

TOSHI-NO-ICHI or Year-End Market
At TOKYO, Taito-ku, Asakusa Kannon Temple. Tokyo Prefecture.

At these year-end fairs may be found everything needed for the year's end and New Year's holiday season. They are fascinating markets to see, whether in Tokyo or other cities and towns, and are well worth a visit. In Tokyo, the first annual year-end fair or market takes place at Hachiman Shrine (about December 14 and 15), followed by that of the Kannon Temple in Asakusa; other fairs are held at Atago, Minato-ku, on December 23 and 24, and at the Kirakawa Tenjin Shrine, Chiyoda-ku, Tokyo, on December 25 and 26.

December 22

TOJI or Winter Solstice

This period is observed in many shrines throughout Japan. Toji marks the time when the days begin to grow longer, the nights shorter. The earliest mention of the celebration of this time was mentioned in records of Emperor Shomu (725 A.D.) showing that Japanese scientists at this early time knew of the movement pattern of the sun. The day brings particular joy to the farmers because the sun grows warmer and makes plants grow; so Toji is celebrated as a joyous day. There are traditional customs observed in some rural areas such as: taking citrus baths, eating pumpkins for good luck, taking a respite from work, making offerings to ancestors, and giving servants and workers a holiday. Shrines have great bonfires to encourage the early coming of the spring season (especially at Yoshida slope, Mount Fuji, or Togakushi, Nagano Prefecture).

December 25

SHIMABARA SUMIYA MOCHITSUKI
At KYOTO, Shimogyo-ku, Sumiya Building. Kyoto Prefecture.

At a demonstration hall here, there is *mochi*-pounding for rice cakes to be used for the holiday season ahead. Geishas and *maiko* (young entertainers) participate in singing and dancing..

December 25

TENJIN MATSURI

At кyoto, Kitano Shrine. Kyoto Prefecture.

Last Tenjin festival of the season at the Kitano Shrine.

December 25

CHRISTMAS

Christmas in Japan has a commercial but no religious meaning except as observed in Christian churches. When the Christmas season approaches, there
is great activity in the stores. The Ginza section in Tokyo, for instance, is
festive with decorations, even Christmas trees replete with ornaments and
tinsel; reindeer, snow-covered trees, and even Santa Claus may be seen.
There is a spirit of gaiety as shoppers throng the streets to buy gifts or to buy
items for themselves after receiving a year-end bonus. More and more there
is an interest in Christmas as a holiday season.

December 31

OMISOKA or Grand Last Day

After Christmas Day there is immediate activity as people prepare for the
New Year holiday season just ahead. Housewives are unusually busy as
houses are cleaned; *mochi* is prepared or bought for rice cakes; other holiday
foods are purchased, as well as *o-toso* (spiced sweet sake), the traditional
drink. Houses and gateways and doorways are decorated. Men wind up the
year's business, pay off debts. On the last day of the year, noodle shops are
busy supplying the demand for noodles at year's end. At the stroke of midnight, temple bells toll 108 times. Most people stay awake to hear them ring-
ing; many go to shrines to worship as the old year ends and the new year
begins. (See Chapter 12: NEW YEAR'S FESTIVITIES.)

December 31

NAMAHAGE

At oga city, Akagami Shrine. Akita Prefecture.

After a ceremony at which the shrine priest prays before a bonfire, young
unmarried men in groups of four or five go down the mountain to visit the
homes of villagers. With bells around their waist and wearing straw boots,
they go through the streets, stopping at homes, where they knock at the
doors, saying, "Is there any wicked person in this house?" Even though they
wear very grotesque masks and are strange enough to frighten almost any-
one, they are welcomed into the house, where they pray before the family
altar. Then they are given sake and rice cakes before they leave and go on
their way.

December 31–January 1

OKERA MAIRI

At KYOTO, Yasaka Shrine. Kyoto Prefecture.

One of the noteworthy Shinto ceremonies held at this Kyoto shrine.

December 31–January 1

HAGUROYAMA SHOREISAI

At HIGASHI TAGAWA-GUN, Haguro-cho. Akita Prefecture.

This event is actually initiated in October when two chosen shrine priests observe self-purification for a hundred days prior to New Year's Eve. Villagers make two huge torches tied with seventeen ropes. On December 31, these are cut into one-foot lengths and given to worshipers of the shrine by the priests. These rope-tied straw bundles are supposed to be a charm that will dispel evils or troubles. Near midnight the young men who receive the charms take them to the shrine compound. By the brilliance of these lighted straw-bundle torches, they divine whether the harvest year ahead will be a poor or a good one.

GUIDE TO PRONUNCIATION OF JAPANESE WORDS

a rhymes with w*a*d	ai rhymes with h*i*de
e rhymes with s*ay*	ei rhymes with b*ay*
i rhymes with s*ee*d	g as in *g*ood
o rhymes with r*o*se	j as in *j*am
u rhymes with m*oo*n	

Japanese contains certain diphthongs: gyo, kyo, kyu, ryo, ryu. Thus, Kyoto is *not* pronounced "Key-oh'toh" but "Kyo'toh." The same applies to Tokyo and ryokan, which are usually mispronounced by westerners, in part because the diphthongs are difficult to say.

Japanese is not a strongly accented language, and the westerner is more likely to be correct if he accents each syllable of a word equally. Names as spoken by the Japanese often seem accented, however, and these accents often fall differently from what the westerner would suppose. Thus, Hiroshima is *not* Hi'ro-shi'ma but Hi-ro'shi-ma; Osaka is *not* O-sa'ka but O'sa-ka.

Several systems for putting Japanese into Roman letters have been used, and the westerner may see various spellings for the same word. For example, the word for "drum" may be *daiko* or *taiko;* "river" may be "gawa" or "kawa"; "l" is sometimes substituted for "r." In each of these cases, the Japanese sound is intermediate between that of the Roman letters.

A usage which seems subtle to the westerner but is very real to the Japanese is the long sound indicated in certain places for the letters "o" and "u." For example, the classical drama of Japan, spelled in this book as No, is frequently seen Noh or Nō, and could conceivably also be spelled Nou. The sound of ō is "oh-oh" or "oh-oo," that of ū is "oo-oo." The long mark or other spellings (oh) for the long o in Japanese have been omitted from this book, but will be seen in many places elsewhere.

Many Japanese who do not speak English can read Roman letters easily; pointing to a printed word may help if you cannot make yourself understood orally.

HISTORICAL PERSPECTIVE

In addition to the names of the major periods, year names were given to minor periods; these were of varying lengths. Sometimes several year names were made in one emperor's reign, but this system was changed during the MEIJI PERIOD.

Archaeologists have established that Japan's early inhabitants included immigrants from various parts of East Asia and the South Pacific islands. Ancient Japanese lived in small communities made up of family groups. These family groups gradually became unified until the whole country formed a state, probably about the fourth century B.C. The Yamato Court became the center of this state. The present imperial family is regarded as a direct descendant of the House of Yamato.

660 B.C. – Emperor Jimmu ascended the throne at Kashiwaranomiya, in present-day Nara Prefecture.

5 A.D. – Emperor Suinin built a shrine at Ise, dedicated to Amaterasu-Omikami, the Sun Goddess, the central deity in the religion of Shintoism.

538 – Buddhism entered Japan by way of Korea.

593 – Imperial Prince Shotoku (573–621) issued the *Constitution of Seventeen Articles*, which called for harmonious cooperation, respect for Buddhism, and faithful obedience to the emperor.

607 – The Horyuji Temple, Nara, erected by Prince Shotoku.

NARA PERIOD (710–794)

In 710, a permanent capital was established in Nara. The custom had been for each reign to have its own seat of government. The Japanese culture of the period was greatly influenced by the T'ang Dynasty in China; but in the fields of arts and literature, it began to display its own distinctive characteristics and forms.

710 – A permanent capital, designed in the style of the Chinese capital of Hsian, was built in Nara.

712 – By means of Chinese ideographs, the *Kojiki* (Chronicles of Ancient Times) —the oldest existing history of Japan—was written.

743 – The Todaiji Temple, the largest wooden building in existence, was completed.

770 – The *Man-yo-shu* (collection of *waka* poems) was completed; understood and appreciated by the elite of the period.

HEIAN PERIOD (794–1192)

During the reign of Emperor Kammu (737–805), the capital was moved from Nara to Heian, the present-day Kyoto. This was one of the periods of cultural development and the life in the capital was marked by elegance. The most noteworthy development during this period was the creation of two sets of phonetic syllables, *hirakana* and *katakana,* which the Japanese people still use today together with *kanji,* the Chinese ideographs. The adoption of the *kana* syllables gave impetus to the growth of native Japanese literature.

Historical Perspective

While the court gave itself to the pursuit of arts and social pleasures, its authority over rivaling clans became increasingly uncertain. Gradually the Fujiwara family, because of its maternal relationship with the imperial house, began to exert greater influence.

From 1150 to 1159, Kyoto was the scene of frequent disturbances caused by several retired emperors striving to regain power. On opposing sides were the Taira and Minamoto families (two influential warrior or samurai families). Out of these troubles emerged Taira-no-Kiyomori (1118–1181) who was powerful enough to restore peace. Kiyomori became prime minister and assumed control of the government. Meanwhile, Minamoto Yoritomo (1147–1199), an heir to the Minamoto family who had been exiled by Kiyomori, rose against the Taira, who were driven out and finally exterminated in 1185.

794 – Capital moved to Heian, the present Kyoto.

1017 – Power of the Fujiwara family reached its peak. Built the *Hoo-do* (Phoenix Hall) at Uji, which still stands.

1086 – Minamoto family gains control in eastern regions of Japan. Rule by retired emperors began, and result was waning of Fujiwara influence.

1135 – The Taira clan establishes its influence in Inland Sea area.

1159 – Battle between Minamoto and Taira clans broke out in Kyoto and the Taira emerged victorious.

1167 – Taira-no-Kiyomori appointed prime minister. Period of Taira rule ensued.

1180 – Minamoto family, led by Yoritomo, rose up against Taira family and five years later attained a victory.

KAMAKURA PERIOD (1192–1333)

During the Nara and Heian periods, the government was centered on the emperor and the nobility. With the advent of the Kamakura period, power fell into the hands of the warrior class, the samurai.

After the triumph of the Taira, Minamoto Yoritomo established the shogunate government at Kamakura. This marked the beginning of a 675-year feudal age in Japan. Even the court nobility's holdings were subject to control of the military rulers. The Hojo clan came to power.

During the regency of Hojo Tokimune (1251 – 1284). Kublai Khan, an emperor of the Mongol Empire, made two unsuccessful attempts to invade Japan with his mighty armada, being once defeated by the Japanese and once because of a hurricane, which later came to be called *kamikaze* (divine wind). The warriors who had fought Kublai Khan's forces demanded compensation but the shogunate was unable financially to meet their demands. Discontent ensued. Emperor Godaigo (1288–1339) conceived the idea of overthrowing the shogunate. With the aid of loyalists, he finally succeeded in effecting the restoration in 1333.

Culture flourished in the Heian period. In the Kamakura period there was a development of religious influence; and in the field of literature, a new prose style emerged—vigorous and forceful, rather than elegant. New Buddhist sects— Jodo, Jodo-Shin, Zen and Nichiren—spread rapidly.

1192 – Minamoto Yoritomo established the Kamakura Shogunate government.

1219 – The Hojo clan began to dominate the shogunate government.

1274 – First Mongolian invasion repulsed.

1281 – Second Mongolian invasion driven back.

1333 – Kamakura government overthrown and the imperial rule restored.

MUROMACHI (OR ASHIKAGA) PERIOD (1333–1573)

This was a period of constant strife. Disgruntled chieftains began to rebel against the imperial court. The conflict led to the extablishment of two courts, the Northern and the Southern. The Ashikaga clan, supporting the Northern Court, established a military government at Muromachi in Kyoto while Emperor Godaigo's Southern Court kept up the struggle from the mountains of Yoshino.

When the struggle ended, the Muromachi military government reached its power in the fifteenth century. However, various chieftains began to compete for leadership, resulting in the War of Onin, an armed clash between chieftains Hosokawa and Yamana. It was not brought to an end until Oda Nobunaga (1534–1582) moved his headquarters to Kyoto and set about unifying the country.

Despite disturbances, many of the shoguns were men of refinement and culture; during the period the Ginkakuji (Silver Pavilion) was built, and No drama, flower arranging, and the art of the tea ceremony were fostered and advanced. Also during this period, the Portuguese and Spaniards introduced European culture to the Japanese people.

1334 – Imperial rule restored.

1336 – Muromachi Shogunate founded in Kyoto.

1392 – Unification of Northern and Southern Courts achieved.

1404 – Trade between Japan and China put on an official basis.

1467 – War of Onin began in Kyoto.

1477 – War of Onin ended, but civil strife spread to the provinces.

1543 – Portuguese merchant ship came to Tanegashima Island off the coast of Kyushu. Manufacture of firearms was introduced by the crew.

1549 – Francisco Javier (St. Francis Xavier), a Jesuit missionary, arrived at Kago- shima and began preaching Christianity in Japan.

1573 – Nobunaga instrumental in bringing about the end of the Ashikaga Shogunate.

AZUCHI-MOMOYAMA PERIOD (1573–1600)

Oda Nobunaga moved into the newly built Azuchi Castle and continued in his efforts to unify the country, but before he succeeded, he was assassinated. The task was taken over by his chief subordinate, Toyotomi Hideyoshi (1536–1598), who succeeded in achieving national unity shortly thereafter.

Historical Perspective

Both Nobunaga and Hideyoshi encouraged commerce and manufacturing; as a result, ports began to flourish. Hideyoshi made a land survey to establish a tax structure, and prohibited peasants from leaving the land they tilled. He sought to extend Japanese influence overseas, and sent expeditionary forces to Korea, a venture that proved unsuccessful. Great castles were built during the period, and the life of the people acquired a new vitality.

1582 – Oda Nobunaga assassinated; Toyotomi Hideyoshi took over the task of unifying the country.

1583 – Hideyoshi built a large castle at Osaka.

1590 – Unification of country completed. A mission dispatched eight years before by three feudal lords returned from Rome and brought with them the knowledge of the first Western printing press.

1592
1597 } – Two unsuccessful attempts to invade Korea.

1598 – Hideyoshi died and Tokugawa Ieyasu assumed the position as leader of the country.

EDO (OR TOKUGAWA) PERIOD (1600–1867)

Tokugawa Ieyasu (1542–1616) united the entire country and established a shogunate government at Edo (present Tokyo). The government of the Tokugawa was one of warriors—each successive Tokugawa shogun maintained control over the entire nation while the feudal lords under the tutelage of the shogunate governed their respective domains with absolute power. Another important characteristic of the Tokugawa rule was its national policy of seclusion, which closed Japan's doors to the outside world. As a result of this isolation, Japan lost touch with developments in other parts of the world, but her own culture made great advances.

In the Edo period, the people were divided into four social classes—warrior, peasant, craftsman, and merchant. Although peasants were second in the social scale, they had to endure the greatest hardships, as they were forced to bear heavy taxation and were not allowed to leave their land. The Tokugawa years were peaceful ones; towns, manufacturing, and commerce prospered and a new culture based on the taste of the townspeople flourished.

Toward the end of the Edo period, many difficulties arose in both domestic and foreign affairs. After the visits by the United States Commodore Matthew Perry, the shogunate concluded that Japan could no longer remain isolated and therefore signed the Treaty of Amity and Commerce with the United States and, later, treaties with other Western nations. The sudden contact with foreign countries aroused a spirit of nationalism among the Japanese, and as a result, the last shogun, Tokugawa Yoshinobu, resigned the shogunate and the supreme authority was restored to the imperial house.

1600 – Tokugawa Ieyasu assumed control of the government.

1603 – Ieyasu was appointed shogun and established his government with headquarters at Edo (present Tokyo).

1616 – Ieyasu died.

1635 – The shogunate instituted a system whereby feudal lords were divided into alternate groups, each being ordered to live in Edo for a year at a time, this to strengthen their hold over the lords.

1637 – Christian believers staged a revolt at Shimabara, in present-day Nagasaki Prefecture, and this prompted the shogunate to prohibit the teaching of Christianity.

1639 – A ban was placed on foreign travel by the Japanese and on the entry of foreigners to Japan with the exception of the Protestant Dutch and non-Christian Chinese, who were allowed to trade.

1800 – For the next forty years, the culture of the Japanese townspeople flourished.

1853 – United States Commodore Matthew Perry arrived at Uraga (present-day Kanagawa Prefecture), urging the Japanese to open their doors to trade with the United States.

1854 – Perry returned and the shogunate concluded treaties of amity and commerce with the United States and then with Russia.

1867 – Shogun Yoshinobu returned the national rule to the imperial throne, marking the end of the military rule which had lasted since the end of the thirteenth century.

MEIJI PERIOD (1868–1912)

Emperor Meiji (1852–1912) set out to accomplish the task of catching up with the advanced nations of the West. Using Western institutions, technology, and learning as patterns, Japan made rapid progress toward becoming a modern nation. A constitution was promulgated; parliament was opened; civil and criminal laws were codified and a system of education was established. Railways were constructed; electric lights and telephones were put into use. "National prosperity and military strength" became the watchwords of the era.

Gradually the view grew that Japan must extend her influence for economic and defense reasons. Clashes took place with China and Russia and finally Japan went to war against the two countries. Japan won both wars and, as a result, acquired Southern Sakhalin and gained Formosa and Korea and special interests in Manchuria.

1867 – Emperor Meiji proclaimed restoration of imperial rule.

1868 – The imperial court was moved from Kyoto to Edo, which was renamed Tokyo.

1871 – Clans were revoked and the country was divided into prefectures governed by public officials.

1872 – Public elementary schools were established.

1887 – Electric lights were used in Tokyo for the first time.

1889 – The imperial constitution was promulgated; modeled after the constitution of Prussia, it allowed limited suffrage.

1890 – The first session of parliament convened.

1894 – Outbreak of Sino-Japanese War.

Historical Perspective 1902 – Anglo-Japanese Alliance was concluded.

1904 – Opposing the advance of Russian influence into Korea, Japan declared war on Russia.

1910 – Korea annexed to Japan.

1912 – Death of Emperor Meiji.

TAISHO PERIOD (1912–1926)

Emperor Taisho succeeded Emperor Meiji. Just as the Taisho period started, World War I broke out. Japan entered the war on the side of the Allies, capturing Tsingtao and the German possessions in the South Pacific. The Treaty of Versailles gave Japan a mandate over the South Pacific islands. During this period, Japanese industry made spectacular progress and there was a tremendous increase in the national strength.

1912 – Emperor Taisho (1879–1926) succeeded to the throne.

1914 – Outbreak of World War I; Japan entered the war on the side of the Allies.

1920 – Japan joined the League of Nations.

1923 – A great earthquake hit Tokyo area.

1926 – Emperor Taisho died and Crown Prince Hirohito ascended the throne.

SHOWA PERIOD (1926–Present)

Despite rapid modernization, difficulties appeared in the social, economic, and political life of the nation during the mid-twenties and were aggravated by the 1929 depression. Gradually, the army, which advocated overseas expansion, came to dominate national policy. The influence of the political parties had declined; there was no parliamentary obstruction to the events which led to the outbreak of the Pacific War in 1941.

In 1945, the war ended in Japan's defeat, and the Allied Occupation, with the aim to demilitarize and democratize Japan, began under the leadership of United States General Douglas MacArthur. A new constitution was adopted in 1947, in which war was denounced as a sovereign right. The emperor was acknowledged as a symbol of the nation and the fundamental rights of the people were guaranteed.

1928 – First general election held.

1941 – Japan declared war on the United States and United Kingdom.

1945 – Atom bombs dropped on Hiroshima and Nagasaki. Soviet Union declared war on Japan. Japan surrendered to Allied Powers on basis of the Potsdam Declaration.

1946 – New constitution promulgated.

1951 – Japan signed peace treaty with the United States and forty-eight other non-Communist nations.

1952 – Japan signed bilateral security treaty with the United States.

1956 – Japan admitted to the United Nations.

1957 – Japan elected a nonpermanent member of the Security Council of the United Nations.

Historical Perspective

1960 – Revised United States–Japan Mutual Security Treaty signed.

INDEX

224